the
MYSTERY
of
EVERYTHING

HILARY BRAND

DARTON·LONGMAN + TODD

With thanks to all my local friends
who tested this course
and in grateful memory of Sally

ALSO BY HILARY BRAND

Christ and the Chocolaterie: A Lent Course

The Power of Small Choices: A Lent Course

Not a Tame Lion: A Lent Course Based on the
Writings of C. S. Lewis

Finding a Voice: A Lent Course Based on
The King's Speech

all published by Darton, Longman and Todd

First published in 2015 by
Darton, Longman and Todd Ltd
1 Spencer Court
140–142 Wandsworth High Street
London SW18 4JJ

ISBN 978-0-232-53208-1

A catalogue record for this book is available from the British Library.

Designed and produced by Judy Linard

Printed and bound in Scotland by Bell & Bain Ltd.

CONTENTS

INTRODUCTION

More questions than answers

WHAT THIS COURSE IS NOT

This is not a typical Lent course. Most tend to begin with the Bible and work from it to expand understanding of Christian faith. This one begins with a feature film[1] and draws from it big questions about life and belief that are often left open-ended. Alongside this it provides a structure for individual reading and thought, with two short chapters each week developing related themes, and parallel weekly Bible reading material coming at similar issues from a different starting point.

But what is really different about this course is that it deals much more with those things we don't understand than those we do!

I am trying to redress a balance here. By and large, Christian teaching focuses on what we ought to believe. And it's natural that it should, because that is what people want to know. We want to understand how to know God and how to live our lives.

The trouble is that as St Paul pointed out 'now we see in a mirror dimly'. (Picture a mirror of that era, not glass but metal, dark and tarnished.) We are human, we are finite, and even though we can learn through scientific exploration, spiritual revelation or ordinary everyday experience, none of us sees the whole picture and what we do see is dimly perceived.

And the further trouble is that we want it all explained. We'd like to hear a theory of everything. That is why, I guess, Stephen Hawking, a human being as physically limited as it is possible to be, searching for knowledge as far and as deep as it is possible to go, has so captured the public imagination.

I say it is trouble, this thirst for knowledge, but really I don't think it is. We were made this way, with a yearning to understand, a capacity for knowledge, and the creativity and ingenuity to seek it out. It is something to rejoice in and celebrate.

But right now, even an estimated 40,000 years since humans first began to ask why and how, we are woefully ignorant. As the Enlightenment philosopher Descartes acknowledged: 'There is possibly an infinite number of things in the world of which I have no idea in my understanding.'[2] There is so much in life that is still a mystery to us.

The real trouble comes, I believe, when we fail to accept this mystery. Because then the temptation is to step beyond what we know and try and offer solutions and explanations that are at best simplistic, based on dubious evidence or logic, and at worst, positively misleading. The theologian Paul Ricoeur put it neatly: 'We know only a small number of things; on the other hand, we hurry on to affirm many more things than we know.'[3] He understood that in this regard, Christians are often worse than most. Christians generally prefer answers to questions.

So the rationale for this course is different, best defined by a 1970s pop song: 'There are more questions than answers ... and the more I find out, the less I know.'[4]

WHY DID YOU SIGN UP?

The psychiatrist M. Scott Peck says that one of the confusing things about religion is that people go into it for different reasons:

> There are some who are attracted to religion in order to approach mystery, while there are others who are attracted to religion in order to escape from mystery.[5]

He says that both attractions are valid, sometimes for different sorts of people and sometimes for the same person at different stages of their spiritual journey or emotional development. There may be a time, especially if you are younger or have had life experiences that are chaotic and confused, when you want it all straight down the line. You want to be told what to believe and how to behave. But there are also times, particularly as you get older, when your experiences don't fit the pattern. Times when you begin to wail: 'But it's just not that simple,' and answers that once seemed satisfying become too naive or prescriptive.

At this point, especially if you are one of those who came into the Church to find certainties, you might well ask what value there is in dwelling on things we don't understand. The purpose of Lent is to encourage and strengthen us on our Christian journey. How can exposing our ignorance possibly help? It is a reasonable question and I would offer these answers:

- Because that is how life is. If we pretend that Christianity can satisfactorily explain everything we encounter, from motor neurone disease to the origins of the universe, then we are kidding ourselves. We become wise by facing up to harsh reality, not by dodging it.
- Because ignorance is a scary thing, and realising it can make us doubt our very being. If we are not careful, fear will push us into denial and from there to defensiveness and from there to attack. It is only by facing our limitations that we can ever really become confident in what we do know.

- Because the God we worship is the prime mover, the great intelligence behind the whole universe. And while Jesus invites us to know him as Father, in an astonishingly intimate and personal relationship, if we focus on that alone we might easily lose an appropriate sense of reverence and awe.
- Because Jesus taught that one of the key virtues of the Christian faith was humility – sadly one for which Christians are not always known. If we do not have this humility then our relationships will fail. They will fail from the lowest level of personal relationships to the highest level of public debate. Even though we bear witness to our faith, our dogma and arrogant certainties may well antagonise more people than they convert.
- And lastly because if we think we have it all sewn up, if we lose a child's sense of wonder, then what a lot of life's fun and delight we will also lose.

So please, even if the idea of 'more questions than answers' upsets your idea of what a Christian course should be, do trust the process of this course; that it will bring you ultimately back to deep certainties more strongly held.

I believe that the Christian faith does provide the solid bedrock that we all need. Nevertheless, ultimately I don't think we can escape from mystery. Rather the trick is that from that bedrock we can see the mystery of life swirling around us like a tempestuous sea, and from our safe place learn to live with its fearfulness and even delight in its mystery.

So if you end this course with no more knowledge than when you began, it will not be wasted time. If you end it with more awe and wonder and sense of mystery, then it will be time well spent and, I believe, will reinvigorate your faith and your spiritual journey.

WHAT THIS AUTHOR IS NOT

I am writing at present in some fear and trepidation, because tackling this subject leads one inevitably to science – not just any old science but the most abstruse and mind-blowing aspects of it. And I am no scientist! General relativity, quantum mechanics, black holes, string theory, the uncertainty principle: when faced with space and time that bend and particles that seem to be in two different places at once, I am fascinated but uncomprehending.

It was over 25 years ago now that Stephen Hawking's book *A Brief History of Time* became a massive bestseller – more than 10 million copies worldwide. It has been described, however, as the most started and least finished book of modern times. Well, I *have* read it right through – twice. I was gratified to discover when I unearthed my 1980s copy recently that it contained markings indicating that I did read it fully the first time round. And now I have read it again. Nevertheless, there are vast chunks of it that I cannot begin to understand! I am relieved that even Stephen Hawking himself admits how difficult this is:

> In Newton's time it was possible for an educated person to have a grasp of the whole of human knowledge, at least in outline. But since then the pace of development of science has made this impossible ... You have to be a specialist, and even then you can only hope to have a proper grasp of a small proportion of the scientific theories. Further, the rate of progress is so rapid that what one learns at school or university is always a bit out of date.[6]

As Hawking explains, science is now so deeply dependent on mathematics (and increasingly, since he first wrote, on computer calculations) that in order to be understood by anyone other than a select few, it must effectively be interpreted into metaphor form – and even then it will be out of reach for most of us.

So although this short book touches on some of these big scientific ideas and their implications, it comes with no expert knowledge, and it assumes that most of its readers are similarly ignorant. If you do have a greater grasp of science than I do, I apologise unreservedly for any errors or oversimplifications. If you haven't, then don't worry. We are talking about mystery and it is OK to be mystified.

(It may be valuable, however, if you know anyone locally with both scientific knowledge and an understanding of Christian faith, to invite them to address your group on the interface between the two. I have also put a resources list at the back if you do want to delve further.)

WHAT THIS STORY IS NOT

'Bio-pics', fictionalised film accounts of real-life people, are immensely popular in cinema right now. I have some resistance towards them, especially those about people whose life stories are still unfolding. For that reason, I almost didn't go to see *The Theory of Everything*, though now I'm glad I did! Part of the reason for my resistance is that, of course, you cannot tell the whole complex story of a human life in just under two hours. Especially you cannot do so if the prime purpose is to entertain. For that, it must be tidied up, simplified and prettified, and in so doing, sometimes the facts can fall by the wayside. But there is something fictionalised storytelling can do, that a strict documentary very rarely achieves, and that is to bring you into the heart of human experience, to 'make you feel in order that you begin to think'.

This film is based on Jane Hawking's book *Travelling to Infinity*, the story of their marriage from her perspective.[7] If you read Stephen's telling of the same story, *very* briefly covered in his autobiography *My Brief History,* you will find it quite different, as would any accounts from their respective second partners: Elaine Mason and Jonathan Hellyer Jones. All of us are bound to interpret the facts of our lives from our own perspective and all of us remember the same events very differently (viz the four Gospel accounts).

In fact, even our own perspective may change over time. *Travelling to Infinity* is a re-edited edition of an earlier book by Jane Hawking, now unavailable, which apparently told a slightly more embittered story, coming as it did, when Stephen was still married to Elaine, and his relationship with Jane more estranged than it is today. That illustrates partly my reluctance for fictionalised accounts of people still alive – one cannot fully evaluate until the whole story is done. The other reason for my reluctance is that it is very easy for the fiction to become in most people's minds more 'real' than the fact.

So it must be borne in mind that what we are watching is not only from one person's perspective but also a fictionalised version of that. If you read *Travelling to Infinity*, you will discover a more prosaic and less romanticised account, and one in which the facts sometimes greatly differ. For example, Stephen did not collapse at the opera in Bayreuth, but became ill in Geneva. However, the emotional journey is pretty much the same in book and in film and it is this that is of value to us.

In many respects it is a journey very different from our own, and that is part of its value, broadening our understanding by bringing us into someone else's experience. But in other respects it is a story we recognise. Even though most of us do not live with towering intellect or extreme physical disability, we will discover many struggles and conflicts that we also share. It is this which makes cinema so powerful, in allowing us to use what we see on screen to illuminate what we experience in life.

HOW THIS COURSE WORKS

This book offers five weekly group sessions each with two related chapters, to be read individually, before and after the session. Alongside this are six weekly sections each focusing on five Bible passages, ideally to be used as daily reading material. They are not directly related to the sessions, but in running parallel to them, they take some of the themes and come at them from another direction. I initially saw these as an optional extra, but as I've worked on them I have found them so helpful that I'd highly recommend this Lenten discipline of daily reading for everyone!

Each group session is timed to be about an hour and a half long (but could easily stretch to two hours). Each uses a clip from *The Theory of Everything* to stimulate discussion on the week's topic. These film clips, however, do not add up to the whole film, so it really is essential to have seen the whole film through beforehand. You may have seen the film some time ago and think you know it. I promise you that you won't remember anything like as much as you think! So please, if you possibly can, make a point of seeing the film right through before the course starts, either as individuals, or in a group.

This course covers some difficult subjects, especially regarding the interface between science and Christian faith, on which many have strong opinions. This is not, however, the time or place to rerun the Evolutionist versus Creationist debate, or anything like it. The whole point of this course is that we move into the territory of things we don't know, and treat these subjects with the awe and humility that they deserve. These five weeks of Lent are not a time to be debating theories, however interesting, because that, on the whole, will not take us much further on our journey to become strong and fully rounded followers of Jesus Christ. Rather it is about sharing our life experiences, reflecting on them, seeing them in the light of the wisdom of the Christian Scriptures, and above all acknowledging to ourselves and each other how very much we don't understand! This humble and open-ended approach, I believe, will allow the mysterious Spirit of God into our gatherings and into our lives far more than any dogma or ideological point-scoring.

It is essential then, right at the beginning, to approach group sessions with respect and sensitivity towards each other. This is not to say that difficult subjects should be tiptoed around. The whole point of this course is that it allows people to be honest and talk about issues often avoided. Rather it means that others in the group need to be accepted for who they are and where they are, that differences need to be embraced and diversity valued as the great teacher it so often can be.

It is also very important in this particular case to treat the film's subject matter, real people still living today, with great respect. I soon found when developing this course that participants wanted to know what happened in the real-life story of Stephen and Jane Hawking, and so some explanatory material or quotes from them are included, mostly in the Leader's Notes, to be brought in at the leader's discretion. However, this quickly leads to opinions on their actions and very easily tips over into being judgemental. The difference between using a fictional story to develop our understanding of moral issues and judging real people is therefore somewhat blurred in this case and that is why care and respect is particularly needed. (There is a discussion question on the difference between judging and evaluating in Session 4.)

SUGGESTED GROUND RULES FOR GROUP SESSIONS

- Give space for every member of the group who wishes to speak to do so.
- Speak as much as possible from your experience, rather than at a theoretical level.
- Actively listen to each contribution, rather than think about what you would like to say.
- Respect each other's viewpoints and, if possible, try and understand what formed them.
- Make it a rule that nothing said within the group is repeated outside. Make it a safe place to be honest.

WEEK 1

'Beauty and grace are performed whether or not we will them or sense them. The least we can do is be there.'
Annie Dillard

'Science without religion is lame. Religion without science is blind.'
Albert Einstein

TO START YOU THINKING

The magic of stuff

God saw everything he had made, and indeed it was very good. (Genesis 1:31)

My five-year-old great-niece is staying with us at the moment and she has drawn me a card. It says 'Dear Ante Hilere, thak you for the sduf.' I'm not sure what 'sduf' she is thinking of. Perhaps it is the eggs she gets from the hens for breakfast, the huge bunch of buttercups she has picked, the neighbour's cat she can plague, or the cobwebs she observantly points out all over the house! Perhaps it is the Lego, the toy farm, and the picture books that have come out of long retirement in her honour, the English sausages (she is from the USA), the liquorice allsorts or the carrot cake. Whatever it is, I am getting great enjoyment myself as I watch her delight and wonder at the ordinary stuff of life.

It's something we grown-ups often stop noticing. Preoccupied as we become with schedules and slog, aches and pains, worries and weariness, we forget how much the material world, the stuff of which our lives are made up is absolutely filled with wonder. It is, so much of it, 'very good'. Still 'very good', millennia after its beginnings, despite some of humankind's best efforts to spoil it, and despite the second law of thermodynamics which suggests that entropy, or disorder, can only increase if things are left to themselves.

But are things left to themselves? That, according to Stephen Hawking at least, is the overriding scientific view, that if there is a place for God at all, it is as a Creator who, having set things up, 'allows the universe to evolve according to a set of laws and does not intervene'.[1] It is not quite a Christian view. Christians believe that God, having started up the world, did not then simply withdraw to let it happen. Rather, God continues to be intimately involved in it at every level, especially with us human creatures with our remarkable attributes of awareness and language.

This involvement instantly raises the question of whether God actually *intervenes* in miraculous ways. Many people do not believe in miracles because they have never seen one. This is understandable, though not entirely logical. Who would have believed that a man could stand on the moon, or that a device the size of a matchbox could contain all the information in Encyclopaedia Britannica? Many scientists do not believe in miracles because, they say, God, if there is one, would not break natural laws that he has put in place. But this too is not entirely logical, because if God made the laws, why should he not override them if he chose? It does seem logical, however, that this would be a rare event, because if God created an ordered and predictable universe, he must have had good reasons for doing so. But regardless of whether you believe in the leg-lengthening, walls-of-Jericho-falling, or fine-weather-for-the-church-fete sort of miracles, what becomes very evident, as soon as we really think about the world around us, is that even the everyday way it works is absolutely miraculous! Think about the fine-tuning of the universe needed for life to exist on this little planet, think about the workings of the human body, about the interconnectedness of the whole environment, about the fact that buttercups and spiders' webs are not only functional but beautiful, and it all seems quite extraordinary. And surely even more extraordinary, if it just happened all by itself.

But happen it did, and both science and faith are now generally agreed that it had a beginning – at nine o'clock in the morning on 27 October 4004 BC if you believe the calculations of the seventeenth-century Bishop Ussher, or about 13.7 billion years ago according to the estimates of the Big Bang physicists. And beyond that is a common understanding that nature is constantly being recreated, constantly evolving and renewing. Not only that, but it is a world in which humans too are constantly involved in making it better. Made with our own creativity, imagination and often with extraordinary levels of determination, we are truly 'godlike' creatures. And though sometimes though greed, laziness or ignorance, we do indeed spoil the environment around us, very often we do live up to that glorious ideal and actually make our world a better place. At best, we do fulfil that calling that Genesis describes to have beneficial 'dominion', or responsible stewardship of the earth.

So the stuff of our material world (eggs, buttercups, cobwebs, Lego and allsorts) is quite literally awesome. Of course, it is possible to look at the matter and feel the awe, but not attribute it to God. Clearly this is Stephen Hawking's position and the tension between his view and that of Jane Hawking emerges as a central thread in *The Theory of Everything*. For Jane, her sense of awe points her to something far beyond the matter itself. It is the experience described by Wordsworth, who sitting below the ruined Tintern Abbey spoke of 'a sense sublime of something far more deeply interfused'.[2] It is that of William Blake who talked of seeing 'a world in a grain of sand and a heaven in a wild flower'.[3] It is a sense that the whole physical matter of earth is God-breathed, and a belief that therefore it is possible to find within it an all-pervading atmosphere of God himself.

It is also the view of C. S. Lewis, who seemed to

find this transcendence in some very unlikely objects and events. In his autobiographical work *Surprised by Joy,* he notes that as a boy he experienced a sense of awe in a toy garden made by his brother, in standing by flowering currant bushes in the summer sun, in reading *Squirrel Nutkin* and in studying Norse sagas. It was not until adulthood that he first began to open his mind to the possibility of Christian faith – he notes that it happened while going up Headington Hill on the top of a bus, and that it was in the sidecar of his brother's motorbike on a trip to Whipsnade Zoo that he first acknowledged Jesus Christ as the Son of God.[4]

God moves in mysterious ways. Sometimes it seems that God creeps up on us serendipitously with something that will delight, or encourage, or release. I remember that at a difficult time in my life, it was not in the highly charged revival atmosphere of our church that I found God's touch. Rather it was in the gift of tickets for us to take our two young children to see the musical *Cats.* Somehow in the magic of the performance and our boys' reaction to it, I found something releasing that lifted me up and carried me through a whole year of tensions and doubt.

And it was just yesterday, juggling a heavy workload and a houseful of visitors, that I experienced another unexpected magic moment as my great-niece ran through a field of buttercups at sunset wearing an enormous Mickey Mouse magician's hat! Yes, life is complicated and sometimes tough, but it is also filled with magic moments. The very 'sduf' of life is imbued with wonder, if we only take time out from our adult preoccupations to notice it!

So as we embark on this Lent course, let's hear it for mystery and magic and awe and wonder and looking at life through the eyes of a child!

SESSION 1

The experience of wonder

INTRODUCING THE COURSE

The purpose of the season of Lent, and of this course, is as a time to deepen and broaden our faith.

As explained in the Introduction, during these five weeks we will be trying to come to terms with mystery and how faith functions within a world where there are so often things we can't grasp or explain.

So as you talk in your group, remember that what you are trying to share will have more to do with experience than knowledge or opinions – and that everyone's experience is valid.

(It would be valuable here to read aloud the Ground Rules on p. 14.)

Introducing ourselves   *10 mins*
If introductions are needed, then go round the room with each person giving their name, their church background if it is an interdenominational group, and a memorable interesting fact about themselves. An entertaining introductory statement, even for those who do know each other, might be:

'Something I know about is ...

and something I am completely ignorant about is ...'

Introducing the session
In this session we are going to look at experiences of awe and wonder and also examine different approaches to life: science or faith, logic or imagination, enjoying mystery or shying away from it.

Introducing the film
Our first film clip comes about 10 minutes into the story. This is what has happened so far:

We first meet Stephen and his friends tearing round the lanes of Cambridge on their bikes, and see Stephen coxing for a rowing eight. We discover that he is about to embark on a PhD in Physics and that while he is casual and slapdash about his studies, he is also brilliant. He has just met Jane at a party and announced himself as a cosmologist, something he describes as 'a kind of religion for intelligent atheists'. He discovers she is more traditionally religious: Church of England, and remarks rather dismissively, 'I suppose someone has to be.' Despite their differences they are clearly falling in love.

Show film clip: Chapters 3 and 4   *9 mins*

Brainstorm   *4 mins*
What did you see in that clip that showed how Stephen and Jane in their different ways experienced awe and wonder and delight?

Ponder and share   *10 mins*
The May Ball was depicted as a wonderful, magical evening – something to be remembered for a lifetime.

Take a minute or two to think of one event or moment in your life that you remember as really wonderful or magical (though not necessarily romantic!) and then share it with the group.

Discuss *5 mins*

The conversation at the Hawkings' dinner table points up the gulf that can sometimes occur between those of an artistic and those of a scientific bent. Even if you have never studied in either of those areas, or had any great interest in them, you probably experience life to a greater or lesser extent either imaginatively and intuitively or primarily with reason and logic.

Which of the following would you most want to back away from and which would you most enjoy? Explain why:

- A blackboard ready to be filled with calculations
- A gallery full of Turner's paintings
- A book on medieval poetry of the Iberian Peninsula
- A treatise on UV radiation from dying stars
- A party where you are expected to dance
- Or going to a church service.

Would you see yourself as mainly imaginative and intuitive or logical and rational?

Discuss *8 mins*

Stephen claims that, 'A physicist can't allow his calculations to be muddled by a belief in a supernatural creator.'

Does he have a point? Is it necessary to separate out science and religion as completely different spheres, and if so, why?

Ask *5 mins*

In an interview to mark his seventieth birthday, Stephen Hawking was asked, 'What do you think about most in the day?' His answer was, 'Women. They are a complete mystery'![5]

What do you consider one of life's great mysteries? It can be something big or small, esoteric or ordinary.

Ask   *5 mins*
In the Introduction, a quote from psychiatrist M. Scott Peck states that some people are attracted to religion in order to approach mystery, while others come into it in order to escape mystery.

- Would you say you came into Christianity to approach mystery or to find certainties?
- Or was it neither or both?
- Has your approach changed over time**?**

Ask   *5 mins*
How do you react to the things you don't understand: do you think about them a lot, or back away from them?

Ponder and share   *10 mins*
In a similar vein to the first 'Ponder' question, but taking it a bit deeper:

Take a moment to think of an experience that inspired you to awe and belief in something or someone beyond earthly experience – something that led you to feel a connection with God. Share it with the group.

MEDITATION   *10 mins*
(Allow for silent pauses between each item and short pauses between each paragraph of the meditation.)

A prayer of thanks
    Thank you, God, for those moments in our lives that have delighted and surprised us.
    Thank you for the times when the world has been to us a magical place.

Thank you that even the most ordinary things of life –
a shower of rain, a flash of colour, a smile, a scent,
a box of washing powder – can be to us wondrous
and full of mystery.

Thank you for those glimpses that sometimes come
to us, of something or someone beyond ourselves.

Thank you for those moments that make us feel very
small or very big, or sometimes both at once.

Thank you for experiences that lift us or inspire us
times when 'Wow' or 'Hallelujah' are the only
appropriate response.

Quote

Isaac Newton, the greatest scientist of his generation, described himself thus:

I do not know what I may appear to the world, but to myself I seem to have been only like a boy playing on the sea-shore, and diverting myself in now and then finding a smoother pebble or a prettier shell than ordinary, whilst the great ocean of truth lay all undiscovered before me.[6]

Bible reading

Psalm 8

Leader

In a few moments of silence now, picture yourself as a tiny figure in a vast landscape. Think about just how small you are in comparison to what is around you: mountains, plains, ocean, clouds or stars.

Let the picture expand and see yourself as just one among 7 billion people on a relatively tiny planet, just one planet among billions and billions, somewhere on the outer edges of the universe.

Now picture yourself in time. See your few decades of life in the context of the estimated 13.7 billion years since the universe came into being, and the estimated 3.8 billion years since the simplest life forms began. We tend to see ourselves at the end of history, but of course we ourselves may be just the beginning, so see life stretching out long after you have gone: generation after generation after generation, perhaps billions of years into the future.

> You are very, very small. But you are also very, very amazing.
> In every one of the ten trillion cells of your body, there is a database, your DNA, encoding the uniqueness of who you are.
> See yourself as God sees you: knowing everything about who you are.
> Value yourself as God values you: thought about, cared for, 'crowned with glory and honour', made in the image of God himself and only a 'little lower',
> given your own unique role of activity and influence within this remarkable created world.

Silence or music   *2 mins*

A prayer of seeing ourselves aright
Lord God,
whose vast ocean of truth is more than we can ever discover,
whose reaches of time and space are far beyond our comprehension,
whose tiny particles and waves of matter
behave in ways still baffling to even the cleverest of us,
we admit that often the thing that puzzles us most is the person right next to us,
and our greatest challenges do not involve intellectual leaps,
but patience and courtesy and kindness.

Lord, help us to own our weaknesses, our limitations,
*   our lack of understanding;*
*   help us also to own just how remarkable, unique*
*   and gifted every single one of us is.*
If we have lost our sense of wonder, Lord,
*   help us to rediscover it.*
If we have ceased to see your glory, Lord,
*   then open our eyes once more.*
In the name of Christ,
Amen.

TO TAKE YOU FURTHER

The limits of reason

'Give to the emperor the things that are the emperor's and to God the things that are God's.' (Mark 12:17)

The Pharisees came trying to trick Jesus with a question about whether taxes should be paid to the occupying Roman power. It was an apparently no-win situation. If Jesus said yes, then he was a traitor to the Jews; if he said no, a traitor to the Romans. His answer sidestepped the problem neatly, but also pointed out something deeper, that there are different areas of authority in life and that each of them serves a different purpose and deserves respect in its own sphere.

Sitting at the Hawking family dinner table, Jane is quickly made aware of a certain amount of scorn emanating from family members towards her religion and her love of the arts. It is a sphere of understanding that for them, all immersed in science, does not deserve much respect or serve a very useful purpose.

This sort of scorn is very evident today from a vocal minority known as the New Atheists, of whom Richard Dawkins is the most vocal of all, implying that belief in any entity you cannot empirically prove must necessarily be a delusion.[7] It is the same sort of view once stated by Bertrand Russell: 'What science cannot tell us, mankind cannot know,' and perpetuated by another New Atheist, former Oxford Professor of Chemistry, Peter Atkins, who claims that 'There is no reason to suppose that science cannot deal with everything.'[8]

It's not hard to see why claims like this overstep the mark. If you define things that can be known, as those that can be measured, predicted, repeated, or proven with statistics or algebraic formulae, then Russell is right, but most things in life are not like that. If by claiming that science can deal with everything, Atkins is saying that science should be allowed to examine everything, then that too is fair enough, but there are many things that even if examined are far from being 'dealt with' and understood. There are still vast areas of life in which science does not and cannot offer us any explanation or help at all. Science can define the chemistry of ink on paper and the workings of the laptop, but it can't explain the meaning of the words. Science can explain how the muscles work to raise an arm, but it can't explain whether that arm is raised in aggression, in praise of God, or to make a point. What has science to say about beauty, love, compassion, joy, anger, determination, fear?

It is a problem memorably defined as 'nothing buttery', or more technically as 'reductionism'. Take for example this statement by Frances Crick:

> You, your joys and your sorrows, your memories and ambitions, your sense of personal identity and free will, are in fact no more than the behaviour of a vast assembly of nerve cells and their associated molecules.[9]

Or this by Stephen Hawking:

> It is hard to see how free will can operate if our behaviour is determined by physical law, so it seems we are no more than biological machines and that free will is just an illusion.[10]

Crick, co-discoverer with James Watson of the DNA molecule, knows a thing or two about the behaviour of the human body, and Hawking clearly understands a great deal about physical law, but beware the 'no more than'. If you hear anyone saying, 'This is nothing but ...', be they scientists, ministers of religion, economists, neurologists or any expert in anything, then be careful. Have they made the mistake of seeing only one of the trees and not the forest? And are they trying, with their 'nothing but ...', to shut down all disagreement?

It might also be interesting to ask whether they really believe their 'nothing but' applies to themselves. If Francis Crick's claim is true then surely he would not be in a position to make it, because not only are his joys and sorrows no more than molecular behaviour then so are his brain processes. He has relegated rational thought to 'no more than' as well. And does Stephen Hawking really believe that 'free will is an illusion'? If so, then shouldn't he refute rather more vigorously all those accolades that speak of him as an example of the triumph of the human spirit? In a recent TV interview with Dara O'Briain, he suggested that his long-term survival 'must have something to do with my commitment to science', adding that 'I'm damned if I'm going to die before I have unravelled more about the universe.'[11] But if he doesn't have free will, then however strong his commitment and determination, they would be to no avail.

But isn't it evident that there is a good deal more going on in life than just physical laws? Another Oxford professor, John Lennox, mathematician and philosopher of science as well as an outspoken apologist for the Christian faith, uses the example of Frank Whittle, inventor of the jet engine:

It is clearly nonsense to ask people to choose between Frank Whittle and science as an explanation for the jet engine ... It is self-evident that the laws of physics could not have created a jet engine on their own. The task also needed the intelligence, imagination and scientific creativity of Whittle ... Science asks the 'how' questions, how does the jet engine work? It also asks the 'why' question regarding function: why is this pipe here? But it does not ask the 'why' question of purpose, why was the jet engine built?[12]

Nor does it ask the question of how this jet engine should be used: for war planes, for ever-increasing long-haul flights using up the earth's resources and polluting the environment as they go? These are questions which science itself cannot answer. Even Richard Dawkins admits that science has no methods for deciding what is ethical.[13]

So we see that science has its limitations. To understand life fully we need so much more: religious faith, the arts, philosophy, moral values, compassion, humour, common sense and many other such qualities that can never be defined in an equation or a graph.

Some people have suggested that science and religion are such different areas of understanding that they should be completely separated out and that neither should trespass on the territory of the other. The American scientist Stephen Jay Gould has coined the phrase Non-Overlapping Magisteria (NOMA) to define this. But there are overlaps – philosophy is probably the term that best defines this overlapping area, and of course there is the vital common ground of ethics, when it comes to putting scientific discovery to practical use. So ultimately such a stand-off satisfies no one. As Alister McGrath, yet another Oxford professor, insists: 'Discussion must be had.'[14] This short chapter is not the place for such discussion (though at the back of the book I suggest some materials that cover it). Rather, its place is to point out that all areas of knowledge have their limitations, that science and religion are not mutually exclusive (plenty of scientists believe in God) and that these different areas of knowledge demand respect from both sides.

WEEK 2

'Out of suffering have emerged the strongest souls.
The most massive characters are seared
with scars.'
Kahlil Gibran

'Life, you know, is rather like opening a tin of
sardines.
We are all of us looking for the key.'
Alan Bennett

TO START YOU THINKING

The problem of suffering

*'Shall we receive good at the hand of God and
not receive the bad?'* (Job 2:10)

Last year my friend Sally died of motor neurone disease. She was 43, a midwife with two teenage daughters, and the disease had taken five years from diagnosis to end (the average life expectancy rate for sufferers of MND, or Amyotrophic Lateral Sclerosis as it is often known outside the UK). Sally was nothing if not organised, and nine months before she died she planned her funeral service. She asked me if I would give the address. I was both horrified and deeply honoured. Horrified that someone so lovely and young and alive should be in this position of contemplating her own death, and honoured because Sally was very special to me and many others. And both of those feelings too, I guess, because to speak at all of belief in the face of so much suffering, especially to a family who were not Christians, demands either someone very skilled or very foolhardy – and I was very much the latter.

For the question in everyone's mind at such an occasion, believers and non-believers alike, must be 'Why?' What kind of God would allow the horrible creeping paralysis of MND? I would love to have been able to give a full and convincing answer to such a question, but of course I couldn't. It is my question too. However, I do think there are some explanations to be had. One of them runs something like this:

God made us very remarkable creatures. We have the capacity to choose. We have the capacity to understand the difference between good and evil and the freedom to choose between the two. And, so the argument goes, God couldn't create a world where humans have free choice without creating a world in which both good and evil were at work. If everything were pleasant, if everything were easy, what sort of moral choices would we need to make? Would we need to be unselfish, or compassionate or courageous? Would we need to take action to make the world a better place, or develop our understanding to try and find a cure for MND? If everything in life was easy, would we be any more than automatons, or chickens scratching round in the dirt? It's incredibly difficult to understand suffering, but if you try to imagine a world without it you may find it equally difficult.

So I do think there is a rational argument to be made, but I'm aware that when faced with the pain and indignity of MND – or cancer, or Parkinson's disease, or dementia, or any number of other appalling illnesses – the best response may simply be to shut up, as the ancient story of Job demonstrates!

Often all we can say in the face of such suffering is that we just don't understand. The important thing, though, and what Job understood, is that we say it *to* God. We don't just turn away cynically and assume faith is nonsense and there's no one up there and there's no meaning. One wonderful thing about the Bible is that it shows us it's okay to tell God how we feel. The book of Psalms in particular is full of cries from people who just didn't understand what God was up to and were prepared to tell him so.

Round about the time Sally was first diagnosed, I

organised a sort of meditative service at our church, on the theme of life as a journey. At each of the different prayer stations was a verse from the Bible, and people were invited to take a copy of this away with them. One of them was from the very familiar Psalm 23: *'Even if I go through the deepest darkness, I will not be afraid, Lord, for you are with me.'*[1] Sally took this little sheet home and stuck it on her fridge. When I visited and saw it there for weeks and months afterwards, I began to get a little worried. It's all very well to give someone a comforting text, but when they're going through shadows as deep and dark as Sally's, what if it turns out to be false comfort?

I need not have worried. At her funeral another friend read some words that Sally had prepared especially for this purpose. Nine months before she died, she dictated:

> During this time my Christian faith has been tried, tested and pummelled, yet despite the odd waver along the way, I know that God has been there throughout and I feel so wowed by his amazing grace. I wish everyone could feel as in awe as I did on the evening I dictated this.

Sally did not always feel 'wowed'. She was an ordinary, honest person who felt anxieties for her family, frustrations with health-service provision, and a struggle with daily living that felt like an endless slog up a steep mountain – and yes, sometimes God seemed absent. But mostly she was aware of God's presence with her and carried in herself a peace and gratitude that spilled over to all who visited. So though I cannot explain suffering, seeing Sally's experience and that of many other believers like her, I can affirm that where there is trust in God, suffering can be transformed.

In 2009 a group of atheists (Richard Dawkins again), backed by the British Humanist Association, started what was called the Atheist Bus Campaign. Several London buses could be seen with the slogan 'There's probably no god. Now stop worrying and enjoy your life.'

Quite apart from the many ironies contained in that 'probably', the slogan has another word that to writer Francis Spufford is an absurdity.

> I'm sorry – *enjoy* your life? ... Enjoyment is great. The more enjoyment the better. But enjoyment is *one emotion* ... Life just isn't unanimous like that ... The implication of the bus slogan is that enjoyment would be your natural state if you weren't being worried by us believers and our hell-fire preaching. Take away the malignant threat of God-talk and you would revert to continuous pleasure under cloudless skies. What's so wrong with this apart from being total bollocks?

Spufford describes some of the desperate Londoners who might see this bus pass by, some of the many trapped by poverty, addiction, illness and fear, for whom enjoyment is just a dream.

> Let's be clear about the emotional logic of the bus's message. It amounts to a denial of hope or consolation, on any but the most chirpy, squeaky, bubble-gummy reading of the human condition. St Augustine called this kind of thing 'cruel optimism' fifteen hundred years ago and it's still cruel.[2]

No, life is not all enjoyment. There's some tough stuff going on out there and very few of us are going to escape it completely. So the Christian message, unlike the atheist one, acknowledges this toughness and tells us that there is hope and consolation. It tells the extraordinary story of a God who suffers with us – and for us. No, we can't explain it. Yes, we can and should rail against it sometimes – God's shoulders are broad enough to take it. In fact, perhaps it's only after we've railed at God a bit that out of the painful silence will come the awe. Only then we can begin to say: '*Father, we don't understand you, but we trust you,*' and go on to discover that God does not forsake us.

SESSION 2

The enigma of weakness

Ask *5 mins*
Any feedback or thoughts from previous session or reading material?

Introducing this session
In this session we are looking at issues of physical suffering, and of living within the confines of time.

Introducing the film
Our next film clip starts about half an hour into the film.

Stephen has discovered his increasing paralysis and received the shattering diagnosis of motor neurone disease. He has been given two years to live. Stephen slumps into despair and tries to cut Jane out of his life, but she is determined not to let him go, and aided by her love he begins to find hope.

Ask *5 mins*
Has anyone had any experience of motor neurone disease or any similar illness?

For your information
Motor neurone disease (MND), also known in some parts of the world as amyotrophic lateral sclerosis (ALS), occurs when nerve cells in the brain and spinal cord called motor neurones stop working properly. It progressively damages parts of the nervous system,

leading to muscle weakness and eventual paralysis. It is not painful but progressively affects gripping, walking, speaking, swallowing and breathing. What causes the disease is not known and no cure has been found.

It affects two people in every 100,000 in the UK, mostly aged over 40. The most usual survival rate is two to five years from first diagnosis, with one in 20 living ten years or more. Stephen Hawking, who was diagnosed 50 years ago at the age of 21, is an exception whose survival has baffled medical experts.

Show film clip: Chapters 7 and 8   *12 mins*

Brainstorm   *8 mins*
The film clip begins with Stephen announcing that he wants to study time, and Jane being told that his time is going to be very short.

List all the ways – from the big scientific picture to our daily lives in which our experience of time is mysterious.

Discuss   *8 mins*
Stephen's father tries to warn Jane off her relationship with Stephen, telling her that 'Science is against you. And it's not going to be a fight, Jane, it's going to be a very heavy defeat. For all of us.'

Is Stephen's father being realistic or defeatist?

Ponder and share   *10 mins*
If someone who had just been diagnosed with a terrible illness like MND asked you why God allowed suffering like this, what would you say?

What would you *not* say?

Ask *4 mins*

Jane is determined to fight Stephen's illness.

What weapons does she have?

Brainstorm *5 mins*

In the next few minutes of the film we do indeed see a fight going on. There are some wonderful triumphs: marriage, a baby, Stephen receiving his doctorate and being congratulated on his brilliance. But we also watch the disease getting the upper hand, as Stephen needs first sticks, then a wheelchair and a bed downstairs. We also hear the tragic deterioration in his speech.

List the emotions we see in Stephen, Jane and their friends during this process.

Ponder and share *10 mins*

For all of us, at some point in our lives, sooner or later, the weakness of our bodies will limit us. Take a moment of silence to think about any time in your life when you have experienced physical weakness and limitation and then share your experiences.

What if anything did this experience teach you?

What if anything lifted you up and helped you to carry on?

Discuss *5 mins*

Some in the group may have had or are still having the experience of being a carer to someone with disability or weakness.

If that is your experience, what have been the most difficult and frustrating things about it? What has helped you survive the experience?

Ask *4 mins*

If you have been through a time of weakness or difficulty, or a time as a carer, how have others helped when you needed it?

Is there any way you would have liked help, especially from the church?

(Supplementary questions to use if time)

Ask *4 mins*

If you could be told how long your life would be and when it would end, would you want to know?

Ponder and share *5 mins*

If you were given only a couple of years to live, what would you want to do with the time?

MEDITATION *10 mins*

Leader

We are finite creatures, bounded by time, and therefore limited by finite understanding. We are like people living in the shadows, unable to see the glorious light beyond time. We may not understand why suffering comes to us, but we can trust that God will lighten our darkness and be there for us as we go through it.

(Light central candle)

Bible reading
Isaiah 43:1–7

All

Father, we may not understand you, but we trust you.

A prayer for those who suffer

Lord, we pray for those who are journeying through a place of deep darkness.

May they see the light ahead of them to which they travel.

May they hear your footsteps steadily alongside them.

May they feel your hand clasp theirs in times of fear.

Lord, when times are really bad we pray that you will lift them up and carry them.

All

Father, we may not understand you, but we trust you.

A prayer for carers

Lord, we pray for those whose life is bound up by caring,

day on day, week on week, tending to the needs of another.

May they too feel you alongside them, encouraging, guiding.

May they find times of rest and relief from their task.

May they find others to care for them.

All

Father, we may not understand you, but we trust you.

Leader

In the silence now, think of someone known to you who is going through a dark time. Each in turn come and light a candle for the person on your mind. As you do so, speak a word or two describing what you pray for that person. It could be an attribute like peace or courage, or a request for something practical: a wheelchair, appropriate care etc.

All

Father, we may not understand you, but we trust you.

Leader

We are finite creatures, bounded by time, and therefore subject to death and decay. But as we look at the natural world we see a pattern: that that which falls to the ground rises again to form new life. And so it is with us, this earthly life is only a prelude to a new life, so much better than what we know now.

Bible reading

2 Corinthians 5:1–8

All

Father, we may not understand you, but we trust you.
We trust you for our lives on this earth, whatever may befall.
We trust you for a life to come: far more wonderful than we can imagine.
We trust you for ourselves and for those we love.
In the name of Christ, Amen.

TO TAKE YOU FURTHER

The leap of faith

For I know that my Redeemer lives.
(Job 19:25)

At the end of this week's film clip, we saw Stephen having a moment of inspiration. Cleverly depicted as the blurred images of light he sees when he fails to lift his sweater over his head, he begins to visualise the beginnings of the universe. It is the moment of an intuitive leap which he himself acknowledges as leading to his work on spacetime singularities (black holes to you and me) and his first breakthrough in the scientific quest for a 'theory of everything' (the unifying of understanding of the very large: general relativity, and the very small: quantum physics).

The film alludes at several points to the tension between Stephen's atheism and Jane's faith, a tension she makes clearer in her book, adding that it was one Stephen stubbornly refused to discuss.

> Stephen usually grinned at the mention of religious faith and belief, although on one historic occasion he actually made the startling concession that, like religion, his own science of the universe required such a leap.[3]

In the realms of scientific theory it is always necessary to begin with an intuitive choice, and then invest time and energy working to prove it – an exercise which always contains the possibility of being wrong. So for the scientist it is, as much as for the religious believer, an exercise of faith.

Of course, forever pursuing his militant atheism, Richard Dawkins is having none of this:

Faith is the great cop-out, the great excuse to evade the need to think and evaluate evidence.[4]

But what Dawkins is talking about is *blind faith*: 'It [faith] means blind trust, in the absence of evidence, even in the teeth of evidence.'[5] Yes, there are Christians whose faith might fit this description, and those Dawkins is tilting at are the extreme campaigners for Creationism, but this does not describe the position of the vast majority of Christian believers (or indeed of all advocates of 'Intelligent Design').

Perhaps the best definition of faith I have found is drawn from philosopher Søren Kierkegaard: 'Faith is a passionate commitment made in objective uncertainty.'[6] By this definition, faith is present in the adoption of almost any belief, and in almost every big life decision: marriage for example – as it certainly was when Jane decided to marry Stephen Hawking. Professor Keith Ward, a theologian working on the interface between science and religion and a one-time atheist, describes the process of faith thus:

You cannot be certain, you might be wrong, but you weigh things up. The evidence is relevant, but it doesn't compel you. There are pointers, indicators, evidence – strong enough to base a commitment on. Faith is based on the evidence of personal experience. Faith is far from blind, it often involves difficult decisions.[7]

Alister McGrath, also now a theologian and previously an atheist scientist, points out that atheism itself is a faith position and in his experience 'actually not a very good one'.[8]

The received wisdom that most scientists are atheists turns out to be very far from the truth. In 1916 a survey was done of biologists, physicists and mathematicians asking whether they believed in a God who actively communicates with humankind. About 40 per cent replied that they did. In 1997 the same survey was repeated verbatim, and to the surprise of the researchers, the percentage remained almost exactly the same.[9]

If you look at the great scientists of history, Galileo, Kepler, Newton, Boyle and Maxwell, to name but a few, you will find that most retained their passionate commitment to both God and to science. If you look at scientists today you will find very many names in the top ranking of the scientific world who count themselves as Christian believers. To select just a few is an invidious process, but to give you an idea: alongside the already mentioned mathematician John Lennox and head of the Human Genome Project Francis Collins, can be ranked geneticist Sam Berry, particle physicist Russell Stannard and theoretical physicist John Polkinghorne, all of whom have written clearly about science and faith. (For a much more comprehensive list, Google 'Christian thinkers in Science' and Wikipedia will give you a long list of names through the centuries.[10])

So faith and scientific thinking are not at war with each other and the leap of faith is an integral part of any great advance in human understanding – and indeed any practical improvement of the human condition. A look at the life of Stephen Hawking makes clear that it does not depend simply on the great thinker themselves. Reading both Jane and Stephen Hawking's accounts, it is evident that his massive scientific achievements could not have come about without the faith of others, notably

Jane. In *My Brief History*, Hawking writes that meeting Jane 'gave me something to live for', both in lifting the emotional cloud that his diagnosis had cast and in very practical matters:

> If I were to get married, I had to get a job and to get a job I had to finish my PhD. I therefore started working for the first time in my life. To my surprise I found I liked it.[11]

And of course, Jane's has not been the only 'passionate commitment in the face of objective uncertainty' that has allowed Hawking to continue his work. It has come from a legion of others: funders, carers, the academic establishment and the providers of aids like his famous voice synthesiser.

Arguably the leaps of faith that most benefit the world are not those of the great thinkers, but of the ordinary little people who commit to loving and caring with no certainty as to the outcome. It applies to every marriage and every act of parenting. And it comes very often from a prior leap of faith in a loving God. Faith is a risky business – as Paul Tillich has pointed out, 'Doubt is not the opposite of faith; it is one element of faith.'[12] There is no avoiding uncertainty – and uncertainty is difficult.

And when it comes to faith in God, the jump can be huge and scary. It moves from the very safe belief that there might be a God up there, through the understanding that this God relates personally to the humans he has created, to the realisation that this is therefore a life-changing matter, and a leap of personal trust and commitment is required. Leading scientist Francis Collins, mentioned earlier, was brought up as a free-thinker and became an atheist for some years, before discovering the difference Christian faith brought to the patients he was treating. It was the words of a poem that identified for him the dilemma he was facing:

Between the probably and the proved there yawns
A gap. Afraid to jump, we stand absurd ...
Our only hope: to leap into the Word
That opens up the shuttered universe.[13]

Collins took the leap and went on to discover not only
the personal God who helps in life's crises, but also as
he worked at decoding DNA, more of the mysterious
wonder of the great Creator God.

Strangely, it is often in taking this leap that mystery
and certainty come together, as Job demonstrated when
out of the mystery of his deep suffering suddenly came
his great leap of faith and certainty: 'I know that my
Redeemer lives'!

WEEK 3

'The journey of life is not paved in blacktop;
it is not brightly lit, it has no road signs.
It is a rocky path through the wilderness.'
M. Scott Peck

'One of the greatest tragedies of our time is the
impression that has been created that science
and religion have to be at war.'
Francis Collins

TO START YOU THINKING

The need for dignity

'I do not call you servants ... but I have called you friends.' (John 15:15)

If you read Stephen Hawking's autobiographical work *My Brief History*, you will discover that it is indeed very brief as regards personal matters. He talks very little about marriage and family and even less about his illness, beyond the bald facts. You get the impression that here is someone who wants to keep his private life firmly under wraps.

One thing especially struck me as I read. At no point does he give Jane credit for all the personal care she gave him. I noticed this in particular, as I had also been reading two other accounts by people with MND: the Revd Michael Wenham, who has written a book, *My Donkey Body,* about his experience, and Chris Woodhead, one-time Chief Inspector of Schools and latterly a columnist for the *Daily Telegraph* and the *Sunday Times*. Woodhead, who died of MND in June 2015, nine years after being diagnosed, credits his wife as the reason he survived as long as he did. He wrote: 'I cannot imagine anyone who could be more selfless and loving in their care for me.'[1] Wenham, who speaks much of his wife's devotion, wrote a poem about his feelings as he sat frustrated, watching her do all the work:

I see my wife, skivvying
The fresh bloom battered by unlooked-for whirlwinds
Is this service, or is it slavery?
It wasn't in the brochures ...
Yes it was. Look here sir, in the small print
No guarantee. 'Better or worse.'[2]

Does the absence of such appreciation in Hawking's writing mean he really didn't notice the care Jane gave him? Obviously I don't know, but I doubt it. But what I wonder is this: did he feel it necessary, in order to keep his dignity intact, to avoid acknowledging the reality of his all-encompassing physical dependency? If so, the reason is understandable. For a man with a proud and independent spirit, to see himself as permanently wearing a big label saying 'DISABLED' must feel very demeaning. Who could blame him for wanting to be seen as a scientist and not just a figure in a wheelchair?

But when you move to Jane Hawking's understanding of the situation, the viewpoint is very different. She married Stephen with the expectation that his life would be very short, but 20 years later he was still very much alive. In her book, she assesses the situation thus:

Intellectually Stephen was a towering giant who always insisted on his own infallibility and to whose genius I would always defer; bodily he was as helpless and dependent as either of the children had been when newborn. The functions I fulfilled for him were all those of a mother looking after a small child.[3]

Her own academic career put completely to one side, her life had become totally consumed by providing his physical care, plus looking after their two children. And as Stephen went on to triumphant success, gaining more and more plaudits and awards, she came to feel more and more invisible and less and less valued.

It was not just the problems of disability that created this sensation. She describes how very early on in their marriage, attending a summer school for physicists at Cornell University, she observed how all the wives were 'scarcely noticed' – they had become 'physics widows'. She described it later as battling against 'the irresistible goddess, Physics, who deprived children of their fathers and wives of their husbands'. She also points out that Einstein's wife had cited Physics as the third party when she sued for divorce![4]

A tiny incident that happened much later, in 1989 when Stephen was honoured by the Queen, also expresses how much she felt this demeaning sense of being invisible. After the visit to Buckingham Palace, the family had lunch at the Hilton, where she was presented with an enormous bouquet of flowers by the management. 'Although it came from a commercial institution ... the gesture was quite affecting ... It told me that somebody had noticed me.'[5]

Stephen Hawking found value for his life in the pursuit of physics. Was that selfishness, a noble quest for understanding, or the unavoidable single-mindedness of genius? Jane Hawking found someone who noticed and valued her in Jonathan Hellyer Jones. Was their relationship unwise, a precious gift necessary for the family's survival, or just inevitable and unpredictable human attraction? It is not ours to say. But it does perhaps illustrate how the natural human craving for dignity can often create complex and sometimes hurtful personal relationships.

All of us human beings need to feel noticed and valued. All of us need to feel a sense of our own dignity and worth. We all need to feel appreciation and respect. But often so desperate are we to fill our own inner ache, to pursue our own dream, to gain our own dignity that we try and do it at the expense of others. It may be deliberately or unwittingly; it may not be in actions that put others down, probably more often by simply not noticing them at all.

I can think of just one human who was confident enough in himself to live without being valued by others – Jesus of Nazareth. But that was only possible because he knew himself to be not just human but also the Son of God. He was able to take on the world's rejection, because he knew himself fully loved, fully known and fully given dignity by God – a God whom he spoke of as Father. He told his followers that this Father was their Father too, that they were all bound together: he was in the Father and they were in him. He told them they were not just his followers or his servants, but his friends.[6] And this knowledge was to turn them from scared and confused to brave and outspoken. They had been given a dignity and a value.

It is a dignity and value that continues to be discovered by Christian followers down the ages, and it comes paradoxically by letting go of our own attempts to grab it for ourselves. I believe this is what Jesus meant when he said that 'those who lose their life will save it';[7] that it is possible that in surrendering our lives to God, we receive a dignity and value that does not come at the expense of robbing others of theirs. It is a different and much deeper dignity, one not depending on our own strength or achievement.

I believe in this dignity and value, because I have experienced it. At times in my life when I felt uncertain, undervalued and unnoticed, so often something remarkable came along to lift me up. But before I sound too ultra-holy, I must point out that this remarkable something has very rarely been a message direct from God! Most often it has been in an appreciative word, a moment of attentiveness, an act of generosity, or a gesture of respect from friend or stranger. God does come to us, but most often through others. And that means, of course, that those of us who have received this sense of dignity have a responsibility to pass it on.

SESSION 3

The complexity of relationships

Ask *5 mins*
Any feedback or thoughts about the material so far or on last week's session?

Introducing the session
This week the parts of the story we are covering lead us to three main discussion topics:

- The complexity of relationships and problems of our human vulnerability
- The conflict between science and religion
- Questions relating to assisted dying and the possibility of miracles.

Not much to cover there then!

Introducing film clip 1
We have two film clips today and the first one moves the action to 1977 when Jane meets Jonathan Hellyer Jones. She and Stephen have now been married for 12 years. Stephen's career and fame is taking off, but with two children and Stephen's now extreme disability, Jane is becoming overwhelmed by the demands on her. (See Week 3, To Start You Thinking, p.54.) Exhausted and starved of affection, she begins to feel she can't go on. She describes her emotional state as:

A brittle, empty shell, alone and vulnerable, restrained

only by the thought of my children from throwing myself in the river, I prayed for help with the desperate insistency of a potential suicide. The situation was such that I doubted that even God himself, whoever he was or wherever he was, could find a solution to it, if indeed he could hear my prayer – but some solution had to be found if our family were to survive, if Stephen were to be able to carry on with his work and live at home, and if I were to remain a sane and capable mother to the children.[8]

It is at this point that someone suggests she might join the church choir.

Show film clip 1: Chapter 11   *10 mins*

Ask   *15 mins*
The quote from Jane's book suggests that to her the relationship with Jonathan was an answered prayer. Nevertheless, as it develops, it seems to be breaking the normal boundaries of marriage.

What is your reaction to their unconventional relationship? Is it right or wrong?

Is it possible for God's provision to come in ways that seem to break traditional moral codes?

Discuss   *15 mins*
Time was when any sexual relationships outside of heterosexual marriage (and anything beyond one marriage) were frowned on by the Church and those involved in such relationships were often ostracised (and certainly not allowed in church leadership). Times have changed, but often the Church seems uncertain how to react.
    How do we as Christians react to relationships that are outside the traditional norms?

Is it possible these days to have a code of approval or disapproval, and if so what could it be?

Or should we refrain from any expression of approval or disapproval at all?

Ponder and share   *5 mins*
Have you ever been called upon to offer advice or an opinion on a relationship that is breaking traditional sexual or marital norms? If so, how did you deal with it?

Discuss   *5 mins*
As Stephen, Jane and Jonathan discuss the beginnings of the universe, it seems that science might be able to prove or disprove the need for a Creator.

Do you think the existence of God could ever be proved or disproved by science?

If not, why not?

Introduction to film clip 2
The action of the film moves on now to 1985. Jane and Stephen have been married for 20 years and Jonathan has been part of the family for seven years. Stephen has gone to a scientific conference in Switzerland and Jane and Jonathan drive down to join him, taking the children, and camping en route. Jane gets a phone call telling her that Stephen is in intensive care, and they drive through the night to reach him.

Show film clip 2: Chapter 14   *4 mins*

Ask   *5 mins*
Jane took her marriage vows for better or worse, but now 20 years on things are far worse than she could ever have imagined, and she is offered the choice to switch

off the ventilator and terminate Stephen's life.

Do you think you could have been so certain and so determined in those circumstances that his life should be saved?

Brainstorm   *5 mins*
What do you think the motivations might have been that led her to make that decision?

Ask   *8 mins*
In the written screenplay but edited from the final film, as Stephen has the tracheotomy, a doctor tells Jane, 'It'll take a miracle.'

Stephen Hawking in his writings makes it very clear he does not believe in miracles, and Jane Hawking never claims that it is. Nevertheless, his survival for over 50 years is an unprecedented exception to the normal progress of motor neurone disease that has baffled medical experts. And despite the diagnosis that he would never speak again, his electronic 'voice' is instantly recognisable across the world.

So, is it a miracle? What do you think?

MEDITATION   *12 mins*

Leader
In this week's session we have encountered several situations where human capacities have been tested to the limits and intensely difficult decisions have had to be made. Probably very few of us have had to deal with dilemmas as extreme as this, and yet all of us have had to face situations that have tested our integrity and courage.

Consider this statement from psychiatrist M. Scott Peck. To some it may seem obvious, to others challenging:

Quote

Life is difficult.

This is a great truth, one of the greatest truths. It is a great truth, because once we truly see this truth, we transcend it ... Most do not fully see this truth that life is difficult. Instead they moan more or less incessantly, noisily or subtly, about the enormity of their problems, their burdens and their difficulties, as if life were generally easy, as if life *should* be easy. They voice their belief, noisily or subtly, that their difficulties represent a unique kind of affliction that should not be and that has somehow been especially visited upon them ... I know about this moaning because I have done my share ... Yet it is in this whole process of meeting and solving problems that life has its meaning ... Problems call forth our courage and our wisdom, indeed, they create our courage and our wisdom. It is only because of problems that we grow mentally and spiritually.[9]

Leader

Yet we were never intended to tackle our problems alone. Listen to what Jesus said.

Reading

Matthew 6:25–34

Reading

Matthew 11:28–30

Leader

In the quietness now, think about the difficulties of your life and how you react to them. Think about these promises of Jesus and take them on trust for yourself.

Silence or music *2 mins*

Leader

Others all around us are tackling difficult problems and facing difficult decisions. How often do we criticise others without knowing their whole story. Listen to what Jesus said.

Reading

Matthew 7:1–5

Leader

In another time of quiet now, think of those whose choices you have sometimes judged, and pray for them. You might also like to pray for those whose story we have been watching.

Silence or music   *2 mins*

Leader

Lord, we ask for your help as we negotiate the
*   difficulties and complexities of life:*
for times when we feel overwhelmed,
for times when we face difficult decisions,
for times when we're tempted to judge others
*   in complex situations we don't fully understand.*
Help us to accept our own frailties and to reach out
*   for your strength.*
Help us to see the possibilities in seemingly impossible
*   situations.*
Help us to be people of compassion for the frailties
*   of others.*
and to help them towards the power of your love.

All

Father, we may not understand you, but we trust you.
In the name of Christ, Amen.

TO TAKE YOU FURTHER

The battle for belief

For as the heavens are higher than the earth ...
so are my thoughts than your thoughts. (Isaiah 55:9)

In this week's film clip Stephen claimed that 'What one believes is irrelevant in physics.'

In a sense this is true. At essence, science is based on a method of seeking understanding, usually defined as 'empirical', which depends on the gathering of information by observation and experimentation. It's about what you can see and hear, what you can measure, and ultimately what you can prove, rather than about what you happen to think.

It is also true in the sense that you can be a physicist with all manner of background beliefs; an obvious example being Don Page, an evangelical Christian, who collaborated with Stephen Hawking on several papers.

It is not true, however, in the sense that any empirical research must begin with a hypothesis, something you believe to be true or think may be true, and therefore want to investigate further. So what you believe *is* relevant in terms of your starting point.

For many of the great early scientists, Galileo, Kepler and Newton, for example, their starting point was very much belief in God. It was a God who had not only given them rational minds but set out the universe in ways that seemed rational and predictable – the sun *always* rose and set, the apple *always* fell to earth. They believed in a rationally intelligible universe, because they believed there was a great rational mind behind it all. Therefore it seemed to them that since they had a God-given capacity to investigate and a universe that obeyed God-given laws, science itself was a God-given task.

Obviously, though, if you set out to scientifically examine your assumptions, you have to be open to the possibility that research may prove you wrong. When Copernicus, Kepler and Galileo proved that the earth was not the centre of the universe, but that it revolved around the sun, it upset previous thinking held by the Catholic Church. (In fact the geocentric view, of the earth at the centre, came originally from Aristotle and Ptolemy, Greek philosophers, rather than from any strong biblical roots.) Galileo was tried and condemned for his beliefs by the Inquisition, and held under house arrest, but it is a simplification to suggest that therefore the Church was against science. Deeper investigation reveals that what was going on was not science versus religion, but power play between different factions within the Church. And Galileo never lost his faith but ended as a believer in Scripture just as when he began.[10]

This myth that the Church and science must be opposed was perpetuated in the Victorian era when Darwin published his great work *On the Origin of Species*. A debate in Oxford in 1860 between Bishop Samuel Wilberforce and Thomas Huxley, a supporter of Darwin, has gone down in history as a battle between science and religion in which science won and religion was shown to be reactionary and naive. This view was characterised by an anecdote about Wilberforce's scornful enquiry as to whether it was through his grandmother or his grandfather that Huxley was descended from a monkey.

However, this turns out to be something of an apocryphal tale, put about by Huxley, a militant Darwinian (the Richard Dawkins of his day), many years later. It was not mentioned at all at the time, when the consensus of reports supported Wilberforce's arguments.

In fact, Wilberforce fully understood Darwin's theory and made his objections on a scientific basis that even Darwin himself respected. And many respected clergy of the day found no problem with Darwin's views and immediately gave them cautious endorsement.[11]

Nevertheless, the myth continues that science and religion must be intrinsically opposed to each other. Of course, sometimes they are, though more often at the level of ignorance and prejudice – qualities sadly seen on both sides – than at a level of informed debate. But most often it is not scientific thought and religious belief that are opposed to each other; rather it is the institutions and power bases that claim these ideas for themselves and therefore feel their power threatened by anything that seems to contradict. It must also be borne in mind, as theologian and scientist Alister McGrath points out, that these kinds of power struggles and institutional battles are just as frequent *within* the scientific community and *within* the Church as they are between the two.[12]

In this week's film clip, the word God comes up quite often as Jonathan tries to understand whether Stephen's theories prove or disprove the existence of a Creator. Of course, in the empirical sense explained above, they do neither. God can never be proved or disproved by experiment or measurement.

What Stephen Hawking's original work did do was provide theoretical and mathematical back-up for the argument that the universe had a beginning – a concept that indirectly points to a Creator. Hawking himself seemed to support that idea when he wrote *A Brief History of Time*. His famous final sentence reads: 'If we find the answer to that [the question as to why the universe exists], it would be the ultimate triumph of human reason – for then we would know the mind of God.'[13] But this was misleading, because Hawking had already gone on to posit another theory, that though the universe was finite, it had no boundary. Under this theory there was no need for

God because the universe was a closed system that could generate itself by laws such as gravity. 'Spontaneous creation is the reason something exists rather than nothing,' he wrote in a later book, *The Grand Design*. 'It is not necessary to invoke God to light the blue touch paper and set the universe going.' [14] You may already see some flaws in this argument and they are outlined very well in a book by John Lennox entitled *God and Stephen Hawking*.[15] However, even could this theory be proven, evidence that the universe could have spontaneously exploded into being doesn't automatically prove God wasn't the source of energy for the explosion.

Hawking noted that in the proofreading stage of *A Brief History of Time* he nearly cut that famous last sentence about the 'mind of God'. He remarks that had he done so, 'the sales might have been halved'![16] There is, it seems, an enormous public appetite to understand where science and religion might fit together – and perhaps an underlying belief that ultimately they do.

But there is also a battle between competing ideological groups, notably militant atheists versus fundamentalist believers, which unfortunately ends up having more to do with power and control than with an honest search for truth. I suspect that many of those who perpetuate these battles do not realise how much they have invested their own security in the 'camp' of which they are part, or that it could be fear rather than faith that motivates them.

Surely Christians of all people might humbly acknowledge that no one fully understands 'the mind of God' and that no one need defend God's position.

From this humble position it becomes evident that all areas of knowledge have their limitations, not least knowledge of the universe, that science and religion are not mutually exclusive and there are many who believe passionately in both, and that these different areas of knowledge demand respect from both sides and dialogue between the two.

WEEK 4

*'Failure is simply the opportunity to begin again,
this time more intelligently.'*
Henry Ford

*'Time is the most valuable thing we have,
because it is the most irrevocable.'*
Dietrich Bonhoeffer

TO START YOU THINKING

The pain of failure

... all have sinned and fall short of the glory of God.
(Romans 3:23)

As in the film Jane Hawking utters those painful words, 'I have loved you ... I did my best', the follow-up that we hear, even though unspoken, is 'but I failed'.

The statistics tell us that there are very many failed relationships out there in our world right now. At current rates, 42 per cent of all UK marriages will end in divorce. The most recent figures show that 41 per cent of all adults in the UK are single.[1] Even allowing for those who happily enjoy singlehood and for those who are widowed, that figure seems to suggest, at worst, a lot of failed relationships and, at best, a lot of mistrust of entering into committed relationships.

The truth is that all humans fail, if not in marriage relationships, then in relations with parents or with children, with siblings, with friends, with employers or with employees. Is there anyone reading this page, I wonder, who has *not* failed at some time or another, in one way or another, in one or other of these areas? If so, either you are exceptionally blessed or exceptionally lucky – or maybe just in denial! Failure is part of the human condition.

Of course it is, for we are all finite. We are bounded

not just by time, but by space. We live in a certain time and a certain place. Our experience of life is unique to us, and therefore our perspective and our understanding is unique to us. We can never fully understand the other, because we do not share their time and space: their upbringing, their experiences, their assumptions, their memories, their fears, their dreams. We do not see the world as they see it, and therefore there are bound to be conflicts.

Not only that, but we all fail in relationship to ourselves. We all fail to live up to our own expectations. Of course we do, for being finite, being bound by a physical body with all its weaknesses – its lusts, its hungers, its frustrations – we try to break out. We are always wanting more, it is our blessing and our curse. The curse is that in wanting more, we try to take what we should not have.

This is what the Bible calls *sin*, and though the word has gathered a lot of unhelpful connotations, mainly to do with control and blame, it cannot easily be avoided. Some attempts have been made recently to release the word from its stern religious undertones – undertones that often have more to do with Augustine or Calvin than the Bible itself.

Frances Spufford has coined an alternative expression: the HPtFTu, or the 'Human Propensity to F**k Things up'.[2] It acutely captures most people's understanding of the condition, but unfortunately is unsayable! It doesn't trip off the tongue as an abbreviation, and in polite society the F word is taboo.

Barack Obama has made his own definition, which, in avoiding any doctrinal statement, is perhaps more useful to the non-religious world: 'Sin is being out of alignment with my values.'[3]

But maybe the author Terry Pratchett is the most down-to-earth, with his statement that, 'Sin is treating people as things. Including yourself.'[4]

But however you define it, there it is: sin, failure, missing the mark, getting clean things grubby, turning good things bad. The curious thing is that however much we understand that this all-pervading condition applies to each one of us, we still have the tendency to make it far worse by piling on blame and guilt, rather than allowing ourselves and each other a little slack.

Jane Hawking was no stranger to guilt. She describes how even when she and Jonathan 'tentatively allowed our relationship to blossom', something that happened only after a long period of time and even then only very occasionally, it was not a carefree experience:

> So sensitive was I to its unorthodox nature that the experience was often watered with tears of guilt ... Discretion and deceit were divided by only the finest line, and it was never easy to judge on which side of the line we stood.[5]

Later she describes how, 'Self-reproach trailed me like a menacing shadow.'

But she also quotes a bit of wisdom from her compassionate and unconventional vicar Bill Loveless: 'Guilt is the risk that comes from striving always for the highest and the best.'[6]

Jane Hawking had tried her best to pursue the highest, even in her extraordinary difficult circumstances. In building her complicated and unorthodox life with both Stephen and Jonathan, she sought to fulfil her marriage vows, never contemplating separation or divorce. She writes that she wanted to follow 'the teachings of our church, which both I and Jonathan believed were the only true basis for human living'.[7]

But in the end she failed. And of course, many others had failed her: Stephen, Elaine Mason, the academic establishment, health and social services, the press, and inevitably also even those who most sought her welfare:

Jonathan, friends and family. Because moral failure is endemic. We are caught in a web of it, both personal and institutional. The Church describes it as Original Sin, in some ways a contested definition, but one that is helpful in reminding us of a situation into which all of us, even as innocent newborns, are immersed.

The reason that the Bible and the Church go on so much about sin is not to pile on the guilt and self-reproach, but rather to show that there is a remedy. My purpose in this chapter is not to explain that remedy, vital though that is. Rather it is to remind us that since we are all in this fallible, frail condition, we would do well to excuse each other a little more. Life is difficult. We all get it wrong. We are all, as Jane Hawking titles her book, 'travelling to infinity', but right now we are finite.

The Franciscan priest Richard Rohr comments that 'Jesus is never upset with sinners (check it out!); he is only upset with people who do not think they are sinners.'[8]

As far as I can see, in my own checking out, he is right. Jesus reserved his harshest words for the self-righteous: the religious elite who were so bound up in the letter of the law that they forgot the spirit; who thanked God that they were not like other people[9] and felt it necessary to remind God of their healthy eating and charitable donations;[10] who were quite prepared to stone a woman caught in adultery, whilst excusing their own hidden sins.[11]

And in the Sermon on the Mount, his great manifesto, Jesus makes it abundantly clear what our attitude to others' shortcomings should be:

'Do not judge, so that you may not be judged. For with the judgement you make you will be judged, and the measure you give will be the measure you get ... You hypocrite, first take the log out of your own eye and then you will see clearly to take the speck out of your neighbour's eye ... In everything do to others as you would have them do to you.'[12]

Of course, Jesus fully understood that once the log had been taken from our own eye – a process that can only be done with help from God and others – we will be far more likely to offer help than to blame our speck-blinded neighbour.

SESSION 4

The encounter with frailty

Ask *3 mins*

Is there anything that has arisen from the course so far that you would like to comment on, question or discuss?

Ask *5 mins*

One of the difficulties of watching a film about real-life characters, still alive today, is that we are not quite so distanced from the reality as we are with fiction. Fiction is valuable in allowing us to enter into different human dilemmas, but when it comes to real people Jesus told us clearly not to judge. Nevertheless we obviously all do think about moral issues and evaluate choices and often do so by observing the lives of others.

So what is the difference between 'judging' and 'evaluating' and how can we draw the boundary?

Introduction to film clip

After the tracheotomy, Elaine Mason is employed as one of Stephen's nurses. She is very flirtatious and tells Jane how wonderful she thinks he is. Stephen is given the speech synthesiser, enabling him to communicate at four words a minute.

Show film clip: Chapters 16 and 17 *10 mins*

Summary of session
This session brings up the whole tricky issue of failed relationships, and from that we will look at our experience of failure in general, stepping aside to ask whether the Church provides enough help for those whose relationships have failed. We also engage with Stephen's question in his book: 'Who are we? Why are we here?'[13] and look at what it means as Christians to live within time, but to anticipate meeting God beyond it.

Ask *12 mins*
In the film, Jane clearly felt that though she loved Stephen and she did her best, she had failed.

Do you think Jane failed in her marriage to Stephen? What are your reasons for your answer?

Discuss *3 mins*
Do you think failure at some time or other is inevitable in human experience?

Can you think of anyone who has *never* failed in life? If so, do you think this is to their advantage or disadvantage?

Ponder and share *10 mins*
Think of a time of failure in your own life.

Did it strengthen you or weaken you?

Has your experience of it changed over time?

Discuss *5 mins*
With more and more marriages ending in divorce (and fewer and fewer people marrying in the first place), the Church is inevitably having to minister to an increasing number of people experiencing broken relationships.

Do you think your church is offering appropriate responses to people such as these?

Discuss   *5 mins*
In general, does your church give a stronger impression of condemnation or of grace?

Ponder and share   *5 mins*
In the film clip, Stephen, again returning to his theme of time, trots out a few clichés: 'Can we go back in time? Will it ever come to an end? Only time will tell.'

If you could go back in time, are there any things you would do differently?

Is it even possible to ask that question?

Ask   *10 mins*
'Will it ever come to an end?' asks Stephen, and at the level of our human lives, yes, for every one of us it will. 'Only time will tell,' he says, but the reality is that within our human existence our story may never be fully told and understood, by ourselves or by others. But the Christian belief is that it is actually only *outside* of time, as we stand before God, that our story will be fully told.

What difference do you think it might make to live your life in the light of a life beyond, when you will meet with God?

How does this affect any sense of failure you might have?

Ponder and share   *10 mins*
'Who are we? Why are we here?' writes Stephen Hawking.

If you suddenly had a microphone thrust before you and were asked to give answers to these questions in a brief 30-second sound bite to be broadcast to the nation, what would your answer be?

MEDITATION   *10 mins*

Leader

In this session we have acknowledged that we humans are fallible: prone to failure and fault, and also finite: blessed by time, to work, to love and to enjoy, but also bounded by it, unable to go back, only able to go forward, and knowing it will come to an end.

Our meditation reflects these ideas.

A failure's prayer

Lord, I tried so hard. I wanted to do my best.
It didn't turn out as I expected.
I'm not as strong as I thought.
I've disappointed others.
I've disappointed myself.
Have I disappointed you?
Yes, you wanted more from me, believed more of me.
But then, no.
For you always knew me to be fallible
and you loved me just the same.
You knew I would get it wrong
and you also knew how those mistakes could be
    redeemed.
Lord, like a tired child climbing onto a father's lap,
    dragging my failure like a dirty blanket behind me.
I come to you now,
trusting that tomorrow the blanket will be clean once
    more
and that you will take me by the hand and lead me on.

Read
Psalm 103:8–22

Silence   *30 seconds*

Leader
'As for mortals our days are like grass.'

So often our days *are* like grass, here today and gone tomorrow, because we are always rushing on to the next thing, never giving ourselves time to reflect on what our days have been. So now, in a time of quiet, think back over your day today.

Think about the things you have seen and done today.

Did you give them your full attention?

Did you value and enjoy them as much as you could have done?

Think about the people you have encountered today.

Did you notice, or try to find out, how they really were? Think about your own self.

Did you fill this day to the full?

Were you too busy thinking ahead to live fully in the now?

Think about your interaction with God today – did you pray for what or who you encountered. Did you ask for grace or forgiveness or give thanks for grace received?

Silence or music   *2 mins*

Read

An extract from 'Time' from *Prayers of Life* by Michel Quoist:[14]

> *Lord, you must have made a mistake in your*
>   *calculations.*
> *There is a big mistake somewhere.*
> *The hours are too short, the days are too short, our*
>   *lives are too short.*
>
> *You who are beyond time, Lord, you smile to see us*
>   *fighting it.*
> *And you know what you are doing.*
> *You make no mistakes in your distribution of time*
> *You give each one time to do what you want us to do.*
> *But we must not lose time, waste time, kill time.*
> *For time is a gift that you give us,*
> *but a perishable gift,*
> *a gift that does not keep.*

Pause

> *Lord, I have time.*
> *I have plenty of time.*
> *all the time that you give me,*
> *The years of my life, the days of my years, the hours*
>   *of my days,*
> *they are all mine.*
> *Mine to fill, quietly, calmly,*
> *But to fill completely up to the brim,*
> *to offer them to you,*
>   *that of their insipid water you may make a rich*
>   *wine such as you made once in Cana of Galilee.*
> *I am not asking you tonight, Lord, for time to do this*
>   *and then that,*
> *but your grace to do conscientiously, in the time that*
>   *you give me, what you want me to do.*
> *Amen.*

Silence   *30 seconds*

Leader

In closing, let us say together the thirteenth-century prayer of Richard of Chichester, a prayer that reminds us of what it cost Jesus Christ to redeem us from our failures and follies, and what our simple response should be, day by day.

All

Thanks be to you, our Lord Jesus Christ,
for all the benefits which you have given us,
for all the pains and insults which you have borne
    for us.
Most merciful Redeemer, Friend and Brother,
may we know you more clearly,
love you more dearly,
and follow you more nearly,
day by day.
Amen. [15]

TO TAKE YOU FURTHER

The journey to infinity

God himself will be with them ...
Death will be no more. (Revelation 21:3–4)

Time was, not long ago, when time did not have a history, brief or otherwise. It did not need one, for the concept of time had been unchanged century after century. Go back a hundred years and you will find a world where:

- You could be confident that time was absolute and that all good clocks would agree what that was. Einstein upset all that by his discovery that if the speed of light appeared the same to every observer no matter how they were moving, then time must be relative.
- Although you knew in theory that time around the world was different, you never experienced it for yourself. Now you can phone your relatives in Los Angeles at lunchtime and discover you've woken them at 5 a.m. Now you can fly from New Zealand to Samoa, for example, and arrive the day before you left!
- You could still believe Bishop Ussher's seventeenth-century calculation that the earth began in 4004 BC, because other ideas were purely speculative. It wasn't until radiometric dating was established in the early 1920s that accurate evidence could be found for the age of the earth (around 4.5 billion years if you're interested).

- You could still believe that God created the universe quickly or slowly, whatever way he chose. Now we have the Big Bang theory, a plausible scientific theory of how it began, expanding from a single infinitesimally small point. This does at least allow for the possibility of God lighting the blue touch paper, though Stephen Hawking maintains it does not need him. But now Hawking has gone further with a theory that space and time may form a closed surface without a boundary – what he describes as a 'self-contained' universe. If so, he asks, 'What place then for a creator?'[16]

These latter two developments, plus of course the theory of evolution, have upset the apple cart of traditional biblical certainties. It no longer works to simply refer to the Bible for knowledge of the earth's origins. Should you wish to continue to believe in a literal seven-day creation, then you have to ignore not just cosmology, evolutionary biology and geology, but much of the rest of science along with it, including many practical applications drawn from the theory such as radiotherapy, microwaves, TVs and computers.

But if you accept that the Bible can't teach thermodynamics and science can't prove or disprove God, then it ceases to be a problem. If you accept that both science and religion are essential to realising the full potential of humankind; if you accept that we're all on the same journey together to discover the mysteries of our existence – then it begins to get exciting!

Because then you can allow yourself to wonder – in both senses of the word. You can look at a night sky and puzzle about how it all fits together, how it came about and how it might change, and you can simply bask in the wonder of it all.

Many of us have lost this capacity for wonder precisely because of time. We don't have enough of it, we say. We are tyrannised by its demands, we rush through life from one thing to another, fearing minutes or hours left unoccupied. But in our stress and weariness, we then go on to waste time – frittered away on the telly or computer games, or just drifting around not doing much. I say 'we', but maybe you do not do any of these things. Unfortunately I know I do.

Not only does this ceaseless rush give no time for wondering about the marvels of the world we are dashing through, it also gives us no time to wonder about our destination. For we are all on a journey that ends the same way. There is a major date in each of our lives, and none of us knows it. It is an anniversary none of us will celebrate. It is an event none of us wants to anticipate. It is the date of our death.

Many believe that on that day we will be snuffed out like a candle, to be no more. But Christians think differently. The Christian hope is that we are 'travelling to infinity'. We believe our destination is a life fuller than we can even begin to imagine, a life beyond the bounds of time. And because it is beyond the bounds of time, we will no longer be bound by physical or mental frailty, or by a finite understanding. In that life beyond we really will be able to explore the mind of God. More precious perhaps will be to know the heart of God, enveloped in a love purer than any we have experienced here.

But of course we are in the bounds of mystery again, trying to anticipate what we cannot know. But while we cannot know what lies beyond, we do need to be ready. If we have met our Maker now in this life, if we have laid our weak fallible lives before him now, if we have accepted his forgiveness and redemption in this life, then we need not fear that meeting in the next. This is certainly the only way I know to move towards death in peaceful acceptance, and I am glad to have witnessed in several of my friends who have been thus prepared, that it is possible to have a 'good death'. (I am aware that not all good believing people have peaceful ends. Some are ravaged by pain and some disturbed by mental confusion. My trust for them is that this is no more than labour pains before the birth or a bad dream before morning, to be swept away when the new life and the new day appear.)

The Revd Michael Wenham, whose book on his experiences with MND I quoted previously, wrote how even a priest, who meets death all the time, is jolted when faced with his or her own mortality. Wenham writes:

> The art of dying – we need to think more and talk more about it. Death is the last enemy. It's also the last taboo ... After my diagnosis I ceased to take each day for granted. I would wake up and think, with something like elation, 'Thank God I'm alive to see another day.' I hope I will continue to feel the same, even as the disease ruthlessly restricts my life bit by bit. Yet equally I hope that, when the time comes, whether it's a struggle or not, I'll be able to accept that life was given, life was full and life has been taken away.[17]

Time is a mystery. But it is not one we should fear. Rather we should rejoice and wonder at it as a precious gift that each of us has received. We cannot know its length and we cannot choose what it should be. What we can choose is to fill it and not waste it. We can choose to spend it wisely in an understanding of its ending and in the light of a future beyond.

WEEK 5

*'I have found the paradox that if I love until it hurts,
then there is no more hurt, but only love.'*
Mother Teresa

*'25 per cent of what I say is wrong. The trouble is,
I don't know which 25 per cent.'*
'Opinionated Vicar'

TO START YOU THINKING

The strength of love

*Love ... bears all things, believes all things,
hopes all things, endures all things.*
(1 Corinthians 13:7)

When Dara O'Briain interviewed Stephen Hawking in June 2015, he asked him, 'Is there any hope of discovering the laws that govern love?' But then he took the sting out of the question by adding, 'Or would that take the fun out of life?' Hawking answered in similarly light vein. 'Women are a mystery to me. That is the fun.'[1]

Obviously, given the immense effort that goes into every word, it makes Hawking's life easier if he can answer questions in one-liners, and with his impish sense of humour he has taken this to a great art. ('I can't sign copies of my book, but if you like I could run over it.' 'I was asked if I was the real Stephen Hawking. I said the real one was much better looking.') It was a shame though that he didn't engage with the deeper underlying question, because as someone who has had far more than his share of dealing with the complexities of relationships, he might have something valuable to say.

But as the sort of question that falls outside the remit of science, perhaps it also fell outside his comfort zone. For love cannot be measured. It cannot be encapsulated in an equation, or tested by objective criteria. Any attempts to divide love into categories are likely to prove simplistic.

That said, C. S. Lewis wrote about four different types of love[2] in definitions that have stood the test of time:

- Affection – the sort of love a parent has for a child, based on closeness and familiarity: a humble, comforting sort of love.
- Friendship – a strong bond actively chosen, between people who share values and interests, based on companionship, but at its best something deeper than that.
- Eros – what is often described as 'being in love', erotic love, always sexually charged. This sort of love, said Lewis, 'may urge to evil as well as to good'.
- Charity – used in the sense of the King James' translation of 1 Corinthians 13. Also often known as *agape*, it is unconditional, modelled by God's love.

But while the definitions are helpful, it is important to realise that the boundaries between the different sorts of love are fluid and porous, as the relationships shown in the film between Stephen, Jane and Jonathan demonstrated.

C. S. Lewis began his book intending to divide love into Need-love and Gift-love. Need-love, he assumed, was selfish, Gift-love pure generosity. He soon realised it was far more complex than that: that helpless dependence is not necessarily selfish, that parental affection can be stifling and excessive, and that charity (especially in the more contemporary sense of the word) can be driven by the need to impress or the need to expiate guilt. Above all he realised that Need-love is a good thing whenever it drives us towards God, for it is in having the courage to express our Need-love to God that we first open ourselves to his love. Need-love and Gift-love are always reciprocal. You cannot have one without the other. Moreover, although maybe it is more blessed to give than to receive, sometimes receiving is by far the harder part.

In writing about this paradox, I wonder if it is an aspect of love that Stephen Hawking failed to grasp. Jane Hawking writes of him:

> Stephen was insulted by any mention of compassion: he equated it with pity and religious sentimentality. He refused to understand it and rejected it outright.[3]

It is sad, though understandable, that he should put compassion on the same plane as pity. The two words by many definitions are interchangeable, but while pity seems to imply someone on a higher plane looking down on another, compassion seems to have more to do with fellow feeling and shared humanity.

The Revd Michael Wenham, in his struggle with MND, understood what it meant to move from a professional dispenser of Gift-love to a position of Need-love helplessness.

> I can contribute less and less. I cannot even help to lay the table for a meal. The astonishing effect, however, I have found is this; as I do less and less and 'just be' more, those nearest me, starting with my family, value me no less. Indeed, since my self-esteem used to depend in part on what I did, I feel that I am valued more.

In learning to accept that others had to constantly tend to his needs, he discovered that this sort of love was very precious:

> First-century Christians had a word for this: *agape*... This is an unusually gritty kind of love, as it does n ot hesitate to pick me up from the floor or to clear up my

incontinence, and it strains and waits to understand my scarcely intelligible words. It clearly does not depend on my usefulness or attractiveness. The only explanation I can deduce is 'because you're you' ... I admit I would rather discover the length and depth of such love by some other route, but I would be mad and infinitely sad not to appreciate it on the way. I have an inkling it's more important than we dream.[4]

So I think that Michael Wenham might answer Dara O'Briain's question much more satisfactorily, because he would understand that the laws that govern this kind of gritty *agape* love have an obvious and simple source in the teaching of Jesus Christ.

'Love the Lord your God with all your heart and with all your soul and with all your strength and with all your mind, and your neighbour as yourself.'[5]

That's it really – all you need to know. Though perhaps you need to understand that the emphasis is so strongly on the 'loving God' bit first, precisely because it is from this relationship with the Source of all love that the strength comes to love your neighbour in tough gritty reality.

Agape love is serious stuff. It is hard to give and sometimes hard to receive. Like any sort of love it is fragile and sometimes breaks down. But if the intent for good is persevering and the relationship with the Source of love maintained, then more often than you might imagine, restoration and reconciliation are possible. It is good to read at the end of Jane Hawking's book that she and Jonathan have rebuilt a good relationship with Stephen and that as a family, together with children and grandchildren, they spend happy times together. In the final postscript to her book, written in August 2014, she reported that the whole family, including Stephen, were just about to go on holiday together![6]

A commitment to travel the entire journey, whatever

it takes, with someone suffering a disability as appalling as MND, takes a very special kind of love. Michael Wenham writes about those, both family and friends, who have committed to travel the journey with him and his wife:

> What makes it more tolerable are those who choose to walk it with us, not because they have to but because they want to; not because they can take the road away, but because they want to be there with us. This fellowship of the road has extraordinary power. There is a mystery about it which beggars analysis.[7]

When we begin to look at 'the mystery of everything', then it seems that the mystery of love – extravagant, tough, committed, giving and receiving love; the sort of love we find at its highest personified in Jesus Christ – is perhaps the deepest mystery of all.

SESSION 5

The hope beyond brokenness

Ask   *5 mins*
Was there anything in the last session or recent chapters
you'd like to comment on or discuss?

Introduction
In this session, we explore the possibility of admitting
being wrong, the amazing possibilities of human
endeavour, the possibility of hope beyond brokenness,
and the power of love.

This week we see the end of the film, which runs straight
on from last week's clip.

Show film clip: Chapters 18 and 19   *11 mins*

Brainstorm   *5 mins*
In the film, it is clear that Stephen is now a big celebrity.
When he is asked how he deals with all the attention, he
replies with a jokey answer. However, all that adulation
must have its effects, not all of it positive. In an interview
at the height of his fame, Jane Hawking once described
her role as 'Telling him he isn't God'![8]

Being the centre of attention and being admired brings
both advantages and disadvantages. List the ones you
can think of.

Discuss *10 mins*

'I now predict that I was wrong.' Stephen is happy to admit that he was wrong – in this case about the time it would take for a 'theory of everything' in physics to be discovered.

Have you ever heard a political leader or a religious leader admit they were wrong?

If not, does that worry you?

Why might it be difficult for either of them to do so?

Ponder and share *10 mins*

Do you find it difficult to admit to being wrong, and if so, why?

What are the circumstances in which it is most difficult?

Discuss *10 mins*

'It is clear that we are just an advanced breed of primates on a minor planet orbiting around a very average star in the outer suburb of one among a hundred billion galaxies ...'

This is Stephen's answer to the question he posed at the beginning of *A Brief History of Time*: 'Who are we? Why are we here?'

Do you think this is an accurate answer?

Is it a satisfying one? If not, why not?

Ask *10 mins*

Stephen goes on from the previous statement to be more inspiring: 'There should be no boundary to human endeavour. We are all different. However bad life may seem, there is always something you can do, and succeed at.'

Do you agree with this statement?

Ask   *5 mins*
Stephen ends with the statement, 'While there is life there is hope' – and in many ways hope is a theme that runs right through the film.

What are the hopes that Stephen and Jane began with in the earlier part of the film that then seemed lost? How have they been redeemed and fulfilled?

Ask   *5 mins*
The chapter preceding this session looked at different types of love as defined by C. S. Lewis. (See p.88.)

What different types of love did you see in the relationships between the characters in the film, and when did one sort of love spill over into another?

What did the film show you about the power of *agape* love?

Ponder and share   *10 mins*
Looking back over the whole of the course, what lesson or lessons will you take away with you?

Are there any mysteries you will still be thinking over in weeks to come?

(Supplementary questions to use if time)

Ponder and share   *5 mins*
Can you think of any examples of human endeavour that
have particularly inspired you?

Ponder and share   *5 mins*
Have you ever had an experience of feeling that hope
was lost and then discovering a new hope or finding the
circumstances were redeemed or changed for the better?

MEDITATION   *12 mins*

Leader
In this course we have looked at some of the deepest
mysteries of human existence, and in doing so have
acknowledged that there is much that we only dimly
glimpse or understand, and much that we still have to
learn. But we have been reminded, through the story of
Jane and Stephen Hawking, of the remarkable capacity
of the human spirit. The Bible tells us that we are made
in the image of God, that we are 'crowned with glory
and honour'. In the following prayer, we give thanks for
what it means to be human.

A prayer of thanks for our humanity
*Lord, thank you that I am amazing and wonderfully
    made.*
*Thank you that I share this room and this earth with
    other creatures,*
*   equally amazing and wonderfully made.*
Thank you that you have made each one of us different.
Thank you that you enjoy our differences.
Help us to enjoy them too.
Thank you that we all have this in common:
*that you made us with the purpose of living in
    relationship with you,*

*that our spirits might reverberate in tune with
    yours,*
and that by becoming more in tune with you,
    we might become more in tune with each other.
Thank you, Lord, for my imperfections,
    for my mistakes, my rebellions, my weaknesses,
    my failures,
    for my limited perspective and faulty understanding,
    *because all these things, Lord, mean that I need
    you.*
Thank you, Lord, for these my friends here today,
thank you that we are all equally imperfect
and that therefore together we need to seek your help
and together we can work to complement each other.
Thank you that together we can learn to
    bear far more than we ever thought possible,
    believe in far more than we can actually see,
    hope for something wonderful far beyond this
    world's troubles,
*and endure all things as we travel to an infinity with
    you.*

Read
1 Corinthians 13:1–13

Leader
'For now we see in a mirror dimly, but then we will see
face to face.

Now I know only in part; then I will know fully, even as
I have been fully known.'

In the quiet now, think about those things in life that still
seem mysterious to you.

Don't try to work them out, but lay them before the Lord.

Ask him to give you the understanding you need, and to help you trust where understanding has not been given.

Silence *1 min*

Leader
Of the many mysteries that we have touched on in this course, we read now about one of the greatest: Jesus Christ himself.

Read
Colossians 2:2–4 and 6–7

Leader
'Christ – God's great mystery. All the richest treasures of wisdom and knowledge are embedded in that mystery and nowhere else.' [9]

The mystery is that we, ordinary, dim-witted, fallible people, with little more to recommend us than a longing for God, can step beyond our limitations and discover that rich treasure for ourselves.

There's another name for that rich treasure. The Bible calls it grace. Grace is defined as 'the free, undeserved goodness and favour of God to humankind'.[10]

'Grace means there is nothing we can do to make God love us more… And grace means there is nothing we can do to make God love us less.'[11]

During the time of quiet, ask God for the grace you need right now.

Silence or music *2 mins*

Leader

As we leave this course, to each make our own journey onwards towards infinity, we pray for each other, that God's amazing grace may be there for each one of us in the weeks and months ahead.

Let us say together the grace:

All

> *May the grace of our Lord Jesus Christ,*
> *and the love of God*
> *and the fellowship of the Holy Spirit,*
> *be with us all, now and evermore, Amen.*

TO TAKE YOU FURTHER

The courage to be wrong

Whenever I am weak, then I am strong.
(2 Corinthians 12:10)

In 1979 Stephen Hawking predicted that a 'theory of everything' would be discovered before the end of the century. In the film, when asked about it some years later, his answer is: 'I now predict that I was wrong.'

Hawking had a healthy understanding that, in the business of theoretical physics, being wrong was an inevitable part of the process. One interesting idea he predicted was that when the universe 'recollapsed', time would run in reverse. A couple of colleagues soon came up with evidence that a collapsing universe would not work this way at all. Hawking realised he had made a mistake and decided the best thing was to publicly own up to it.

> What do you do when you make a mistake like that? Some people never admit that they are wrong and continue to find new and often mutually inconsistent arguments to support their case ... Others claim to have never really supported the incorrect view in the first place or, if they did, it was only to show that it was inconsistent. It seems to me much better and less confusing if you admit in print that you were wrong.[12]

In fact science would have never moved forward at all without a great many people admitting they were wrong.

The whole concept of taking an unproved idea and testing it assumes the possibility that it may turn out to be a blind alley. Like going round a maze, it may be only when you have tried all the possible paths and ruled out the wrong ones that you are able to proceed along the right one. And this might mean that quite a few scientists spend their entire life on something that turns out to be a blind alley, while another may stumble upon the truth almost by accident. The one who makes the discovery is acclaimed for generations and the others are forgotten – which is of course highly unfair since all have been equally part of the great endeavour. All of which makes it far more important that you take up the task because you love the quest itself, and not because of any glory or reward it might give.

My father was a wise man, though in such an unassuming way that it took me a long time to realise it. I still though remember something he said to me, when as a teenager I was busy discarding the faith I'd been brought up in. He couldn't prove to me, he said, that Christianity was true; he claimed only that it seemed so to him and that therefore he'd decided to stake his life on it. Much later, as an old man, he wrote this:

> You ask me why I decided to become a Christian and I guess the simple answer is that it struck me as the best way to live. I didn't understand all the doctrine, but I wanted to be – or rather try to be – like Jesus. That was when I was a teenager and I've obviously got to know a lot more since then, but one thing I'm quite sure about – I've never come across anyone more worth following.
>
> So the Christian faith is my firm conviction but I'm still prepared to consider the possibility that I may be wrong. Just suppose that when my ticker stops ticking and the frenetic activity in my little grey cells closes down and I wake up to discover that all I

have lived by is somewhat wide of the mark, or even total nonsense, will it matter? Will all my thought and study, my prayer and worship be a complete waste of time? No, it won't. Our lives are meant to be an unending quest for spiritual truth on the clear understanding that we'll take a few wrong turnings and go up a few blind alleys.

If it eventually turns out that I've got it all wrong, it won't matter a scrap! My life will have been much richer and more satisfying for having spent years reaching out towards eternal truth, however elusive it sometimes appears to be.[13]

It seems to me that in that sentiment is not only wisdom, but strength. It's the strength of standing firmly on what you've found to be solid, while at the same time looking around to try and see what ground others have found and why they are standing there. It's the strength of trying to fully understand and use what you've discovered from your unique perspective, while always being interested in what others with their unique perspective might be able to give to you.

Steve Chalke tells a story about how a friend of his wrote to *The Times* journalist John Diamond. Diamond was suffering with terminal throat cancer and had been writing in his Saturday column about the experience. One weekend, Diamond noted how many Christians had written to him, concerned for his 'eternal destiny' and urging him to repent. Diamond's response was gracious, commenting only that he was flattered so many people were worried about his soul, and that, despite the judgemental tone of some of them, he appreciated they meant well. But Steve Chalke's friend, bothered by the insensitivity of what some of the Christians had written, decided to write to Diamond himself. He explained how he had been through similar tough times and wrote, 'In my experience God brings meaning and hope to the random stuff that happens in life.' He ended by saying, 'Well, that's my story, John. If you ever want to tell me yours I'd love to meet and have a chat. I really think you could help me in my journey and so I'd love to talk to you about your insights.' He didn't expect to get a letter in return but he did. Diamond wrote:

> The problem I have with Christians is that they are so often peddlers of certainty. You are the only Christian in the entirety of my life who has ever told me that they thought they could learn something from me. I'd love to meet with you and talk further.[14]

Sadly Diamond died before the meeting could happen.

How strange that Christians, whose mission is to love their neighbour as themselves, so often assume they know more and do better than that neighbour. How strange that those whose doctrinal statements include regular admissions that they've 'erred and strayed' and equally regular reassurance that they can be forgiven and redeemed, should in practice be so often unwilling to admit they could be wrong. How strange that people who worship a God whose ways they acknowledge to be as high above them as the heavens are beyond the earth, should so often be certain they understand God entirely.

Admitting you are wrong is uncomfortable. It makes you vulnerable, makes you feel foolish, makes you scared the whole edifice of your life could be falling around your ears. But uncomfortable or not, admitting your fallibility makes good sense. In pre-empting the criticisms of others, it actually protects you from making a fool of yourself. In opening up honest conversations, it brings the possibility to grow and learn. Above all else, it makes sense because it opens you up to God. 'Power is made perfect in weakness,'[15] says St Paul, who realised that when he was weak an amazing power began to flourish in his life – the power of God's grace.

CONCLUSION

The peas and the potatoes

I have sometimes observed, in other writers and speakers, what a bad idea it is to take a half-understood scientific idea and try to turn it into a spiritual metaphor. I am also aware that it is generally rather foolish, when up against a tight deadline, to try and put on paper an idea that is only half-formed and vaguely glimpsed. Nevertheless, on both fronts, I find myself driven to try!

In the film Jane Hawking explains the elusive theory of everything by spearing on two forks a potato and a pea. The potato is General Relativity, Einstein's theory which governs movement at the huge scale of the universe, and the pea is Quantum Theory, the laws which govern the very small: electrons, particles and so on. 'They don't remotely play by the same rules,' explains Jane. 'Peas are chaotic and don't behave predictably at all.' Unlike potatoes, 'which you can set your watch by'.

'If the world were all potatoes', solid and dependable, says Jane, it would be easy, 'Hallelujah, God lives.' But if you try to incorporate peas, slippery and always falling off the fork, then it all goes haywire. 'A godless mess.' This seems to me to be a very good description of the difference between solid spiritual laws that the Church teaches and the slippery confusion and complexity of everyday life. So often they just don't seem to fit together. Yet just as Stephen Hawking tries to reconcile the cosmological big picture with the minuscule movements of protons and neutrons, it seems to me that for Christianity to go really deep in my own life and for it to be credible to those outside the Church, there must be some way of understanding in spiritual terms how the doctrinally solid potatoes and the everyday messy peas fit together.

I cannot formulate a unified theory in proper theological language. I feel that I am only just glimpsing it. But what I am glimpsing seems to be encapsulated in the word *grace*.

Grace in Christian terms is perhaps most simply defined as a 'generous, free, totally unexpected and undeserved' gift of God.[1] It is used at the broader level to describe how all creation, beautifully and intricately designed, imbued with the spirit of the God who created it, is a gift to humankind to bring us wonder and delight as well as practical help and sustenance. This is sometimes defined as *natural grace*, available at all times to all people.

But there is also what is often described as *supernatural grace*, something even more mysterious, that comes at specific times in specific ways to specific people. These people are not particularly holy, they haven't done anything special, indeed they haven't done anything at all, to deserve it. They may be people who are asking specifically, reaching out to God for something they need, but the odd thing is that it doesn't always work that way. Sometimes it seems that God directs this supernatural grace towards people who didn't seem to be seeking it at all. It arrives quite unexpectedly – they may not even identify from whence it came – it lifts them up and sometimes quite 'blows them away'. Within this supernatural grace we usually find the qualities described in two other great words: *forgiveness* and *redemption*. It often comes in response to *faith,* but if faith was not there already, then often it generates it. It is usually characterised by the *hope* that it brings. And pretty well always, I think, it bathes its recipients in *love*. Sometimes they know what is happening to them and

who has done it. Sometimes they don't. They may simply
be aware that something in them or in their situation has
shifted. They may be aware of nothing at all, but others
may notice the change. (I'm reminded of a quote I once
read from a Victorian cabbie, converted by the Salvation
Army, on the change in his life: 'No drinkin', no cussin',
and the 'orses know the difference.')

Grace may come suddenly and change everything in a
moment – what Jesus described as being 'born again'; or
it may grow in a life slowly and unseen – taking weeks,
years or even decades.

Grace hardly ever changes the human circumstances
into which it enters. It rarely takes away cancers, rebuilds
earthquake-shattered cities, turns back invading armies,
or obliterates the consequences of crime. But in all these
circumstances, it can and sometimes does (I suspect far
more often than we realise) transform the experience. It
can, in almost any terrible circumstance you care to name,
bring totally unexpected good out of appallingly awful bad.

Grace, it seems, is unpredictable, behaving exactly
in the way Jesus described God's spirit, like a wind
that 'blows where it chooses'.[2] But then again ... as
soon as I wrote that last sentence, I realised how little I
understood. Surely forgiveness is never withheld, surely
redemption is always offered. Maybe it is the forces
operating against it I don't understand: selfishness,
ignorance – dare I say it, sin and the devil!

Thankfully many great and wise people down the
generations, starting with St Paul, have laboured to
understand grace, expressing it in good, solid spiritual
laws. The language that expresses these laws may vary in
different Christian traditions but the gist is always the same:
God loves his human children and wants to bless them.

There is one thing they all seem agreed on: that grace
is free, but it is never cheap. It comes at a great cost, the
cost of Jesus Christ dying on a cross to bring salvation.
Again the way this works will be expressed in different

language in different traditions, but never the fact that it is central to the whole story. To understand grace, we must return to the person of Jesus, mysterious, paradoxical, but then again remarkably solid and down-to-earth; a person rooted in history and recorded in a book, but also a presence that millions of people down the centuries have encountered for themselves. Someone whom millions of people have felt compelled and thrilled to follow.

Most people during their lives put together their own theory of everything. It comes from their preconceptions: what their parents taught them, what their society believes; from their life experiences: their joys and disappointments; plus from a mishmash of opinions, throwaway comments, unexpressed prejudices, half-buried subtexts gleaned from friends, colleagues, news, fiction, songs, even ads on the side of buses. Very few people ever take out their theory and examine it. Many are not even aware it is there. It is more often described as a world-view, and sometimes likened to a pair of spectacles through which you view the world. Everything in life is seen through those specs, but you very rarely examine the spectacles themselves. Only if your vision becomes blurred do you ask whether the spectacles are dirty or distorting or unsuitable for your eyes. And equally rarely do you ask if your theory is fit for purpose.

Carl Sagan, in his Introduction to the original edition of *A Brief History of Time,* says:

> A theory is a good theory if it satisfies two requirements: it must accurately describe a large class of observations on the basis of a model that contains only a few arbitrary elements, and it must make definite predictions about the results of future observations.[3]

I wonder whether what is true for a scientific theory is also true for a spiritual one, and I wonder whether on that basis we ought to examine our spiritual theories a little more. Do they accurately describe what we are experiencing in life? Do they provide a basis for predicting what our future actions should be? Can we rely on them to accurately show us how life should be lived? In other words, what do we really believe, deep down, when all the religious add-ons are stripped away? Does it really work – or, more precisely, which bits do and which bits don't? (For example, I might assume that to be a Christian believer is a good thing. However, if I examine the facts a little more, I might discover that being a believer and a humble person is indeed good, whereas being a believer and a power-hungry or bigoted person might actually be worse than not believing at all.)

So if you subscribe to the theory of Christian faith (as presumably you do, since you are reading this Lent book), how can you actually test your hypothesis? Well, you live it. You become a disciple of Jesus Christ, with all its costs and with all its wonderful riches. I know of no other way, and so far on my journey of faith, rather a long one now, I can attest that it is worth it. My life journey, I am aware, has been far easier than that of many other people. Nevertheless, it has contained its share of troubles and struggles and within them all, surprisingly, I discover grace.

I know that I never will fully put together my theory of everything. Unlike Stephen Hawking, I do not believe that finite humans ever will, through reason or through revelation, entirely discover the mind of God. Given the vast areas that we don't even begin to understand, it seems mystery is here to stay. Maybe, of course, there is a very good reason why God wants it that way!

However, that is not going to stop me trying. Like Stephen Hawking, I believe that, given our amazing capacity for reason, imagination, determination and leaps of faith, all us human beings, Christian believers and non-believers alike, have a responsibility and a calling to move further both in our understanding and in our practical application of that understanding.

After all, that is surely what time itself teaches us. The arrow of time moves forward. It gets its momentum from what has come before, but it does not go back. Our own brief earthly histories will soon be over, soon we will step beyond time.

So if we are wise we will invest what time we have in something that will last beyond time. If we are wise we will not just accept the Christian hypothesis but test it out rigorously. There will still be plenty of mystery and hopefully we will be able to embrace it, but it is only then we will discover, I dare to predict, that grace abounds for us in every circumstance of our lives.

POSTSCRIPT

In writing this course I realise that I am hugely indebted, not just to the film-makers, who in *The Theory of Everything* created a movie to inspire and provoke much thought, but even more to the real-life protagonists of the story: Stephen Hawking, Jane Wilde Hawking and Jonathan Hellyer Jones. As I have tested this course with two groups of volunteers, I have frequently felt uncomfortable that we have been using the deeply personal and painful story of real-life people we have never met to examine our own understanding, to talk about beliefs they may not share, and sometimes to make value-judgements on experiences we cannot hope to understand. So, even though I doubt they will ever read this, I want to apologise to Stephen, Jane and Jonathan for the impertinence of our intrusion into their story, and also to express thanks and huge respect. For me, those who have tested this course with me, and I am sure for all those who go on to follow it, they have provided massive inspiration. In their determination, humour, compassion, self-giving – and yes, in their willingness to expose their frailties – we have learned so much more about what it means to be human. Thank you.

BIBLE
READINGS

'The Bible was written to show us how to go to heaven, not how the heavens go.'
Galileo Galilei

'Read it to be wise, believe it to be safe, and practice it to be holy. It contains light to direct you, food to support you, and comfort to cheer you.'
Anonymous – The Gideons

BIBLE READINGS

The surprising wisdom of an ancient book

The Bible is a collection of writings by ordinary flawed human beings, struggling to comprehend and then to explain what they glimpsed of truth. They saw it as a sacred task and laboured hard to be truthful, but, of course, their understanding was limited and occasionally mistakes crept in. But frequently, very frequently, revelation was given to them – so what we have in the Bible is a collection of writings shot through with insights that leap off the page and linger in the brain. So powerfully have these writings resonated with human experience, that they have been described as 'God-breathed', first by St Paul[1] and then by many others since. This 'God-breathed-ness', I believe, works at different levels, obviously that of the original writers, but also at the level of the reader, so that as we read – even those passages we find hard to explain – God's spirit is entering into us with truths and understanding just for us. To discover this 'God-breathed-ness' requires a special sort of reading: reading that gives the words space to breathe, reading that comes with no preconceived agendas, and above all, reading infused with prayer. All this takes time. It need not be a long time (in this case ten minutes for each Bible passage would do), but it does need to be time set apart especially for this purpose. So though I have designed these as daily readings, I realise that for some people that may not work. So take them and read them as seems best for you.

I would say, however, that since Lent is designed to be a

time of self-discipline and new challenges, maybe time set aside for reading, prayer and meditation might be just the challenge that God would like you to take up this Lent!

WEEK 1
THE MYSTERY OF OUR ORIGINS

The book of Genesis is an account of life's origins entirely different from the scientific approach. These ancient writers expressed their understanding in the form of myth, a word that to contemporary ears still needs explanation. It has two current meanings, that of something untrue, and the rather different one being used here of 'a story told to make sense of the world'. In this latter definition, a myth may be factual or fictional, or quite likely both, for the ancient storytellers had no methods to sift one from the other. But don't conclude that because these stories may not be factual, they therefore aren't true. These ancient stories have lasted precisely because they do say something deep and truthful about the human condition, and that is why they reward our attention.

DAY 1

'God saw everything that he had made and indeed it was very good.'

Read

Genesis 1:1–5 and 26–31

Understand

Long before the mechanism of the Big Bang was conceived, the Judeo-Christian understanding was that the world had a beginning (unlike the Greek philosophy of Plato and some Eastern religions like Buddhism, which claim life always was). The Genesis writers understood not only that our universe had a Prime Mover, but that this was a God deeply involved at every stage of the process – and enjoying it too. 'Yes, that's good,' he keeps saying, and even speaks directly to his creation: to the earth and its vegetation, to the birds and animals, and to humankind, blessing them and giving them their task. This God was not just a force but a Person, the epitome of personhood, and that made all the difference, for the nature of personhood is to love.

Reflect
Picture God bringing you into being, as no more than a cluster of cells. Picture him saying to himself, 'Yes, this is good', then speaking his blessing over you and giving you your secret unknown tasks. Genesis shows God having this level of love and interaction with all humankind – even and especially you.

Pray
Lord God, help me be the person you intended me to be.
May my dominion over my little patch of earth be just and fruitful.
May your blessing remain with me throughout my life.
May I fulfil the tasks to which you call me.

DAY 2
'For God knows that when you eat of it your eyes will be opened ...'

Read
Genesis 2:15–18 and 3:1–7

Understand
You will probably have absorbed so many accretions to this story, it's hard to see the original without them. For instance, did you realise it doesn't include the words 'apple', 'sin' or 'Fall'? Think about it now, not as an ancient incident for which we bear the consequences, but as a picture of us all: the journey each of us makes from the safety of childhood, through the boundary-

breaking of adolescence to the 'sweat of the brow' of adulthood. God must have realised this was the nature of the humans he had made. God did not want automatons. Rather, like any good parent, his intent was to help the first humans push the boundaries at the right time in the right way. Unfortunately, like all of us sooner or later, the first couple pushed too far for their own good.

Reflect

Have you heard that voice in your head, the voice of the serpent? 'Is that really off-limits?' 'What harm can it do?' In today's world, delayed gratification is unpopular, and gratification permanently postponed an absurdity. Yet sometimes this is what God calls us to. What are the voices in your head clamouring for? Are you sure God wants you to have them?

Pray

*Lord God, help me hear the subtle voices for what
   they are.
May I be prepared to hold back,
to wait to be given rather than to take.
May I think more about responsibilities than rights.*

DAY 3

'Sin is lurking at the door, its desire is for you, but you must master it.'

Read

Genesis 4:1–15

Understand

This is where the word 'sin' first comes in, not against God, but against a brother, not in disobedience but in envy. Yes, this is where it begins – it begins in families: in tiny things said or done or sometimes simply inferred, things that create resentments that if left will fester and grow. Mostly it begins in childhood, because all siblings must at times face rivalry, and no parents (or teachers) are perfectly wise and even-handed. It pursues us into adulthood: into marriage, into the work place, even into churches. Strangely even the most talented and privileged people can be its victims. And as Cain discovered, letting it have the mastery leads only to regret and alienation. Though as he also discovered, God did not give up on him.

Reflect

This dark envy is always lurking at the door, never far from any of us. So picture in your mind now those who you envy, or envied once. Then picture once again God blessing the tiny cluster of cells that will become you and giving the tasks that only you could achieve.

Pray

Lord God, help me to accept that life is never fair,
to know, nevertheless, that you made me and love me
*   just as I am,*
to know that you still work for my good, whatever ill
*   I do.*
Protect me, Lord, from envy. Let not sin have the mastery.

DAY 4

'The Lord said ... "This is only the beginning of what they will do."'

Read

Genesis 11:1–9

Understand

This book of beginnings charts how quickly rivalry spread from family units to tribes and people groups. The violence it provoked caused God to send a flood; though even that could not stop it. On it moved into the formation of city states, and as God looked down on the massive tower being built on the plain of Shinar, he understood that this was an act of hubris. Hubris means excessive pride: pride without the good bits of dignity and rightful self-esteem. Hubris is a pride that is intent not merely on seeing itself as having value, but being seen by others as the best. It is intent on provoking envy and on gathering control and power. It is pride without limitations, so intent on proving itself that moral boundaries are broken. It happens within every organisation and is undoubtedly happening in one near you.

Reflect
In what aspects of your life have you become victim of hubris? Maybe you have been directly put down by another, intent on gaining control or position. Or perhaps indirectly, as the result of institutional corruption, or simply the hubris inherent in maintaining the status quo. Wherever you find it, pray for those who create it or perpetuate it, for they are undoubtedly discontented people.

Pray
> Lord God, help me not resent those whose scramble to
> the top has pushed me down.
> Help me retain my rightful dignity in the face of their
> unrighteous hubris.
> Help them find the only validation that can truly satisfy,
> that which comes from you.

DAY 5
'Now the Lord said to Abram, "Go ... to the land which I will show you."'

Read
Genesis 12:1–8

Understand
It might be concluded that relations between God and humankind have been somewhat strained so far in this

history of beginnings. But now the story takes a different turn, moving to God's relationship with one particular man and following it through in detail. Right from the start God is seen as caring for individuals, even those who made life difficult for themselves, and now again we see God working not in a great hero, but in a flawed individual. (See the rest of chapter 12 for an example.) Abram's story is recorded because it marks the beginning of the Jewish nation, but it has a wider resonance. It shows that God cares not just for that particular individual, but for the complex twists and turns in every individual's life.

Reflect

Picture God coming to you and sending you on a journey. What is it? Is it new, or have you been on it for years? Has it changed over time? Maybe it's time for a new one! Whatever it is, God is with you on it. Let God come now to strengthen or redirect.

Pray

> Lord God, help me take the right steps through life,
>   even if I do not know the destination.
> May I know you with me, even in difficulties I could
>   never have envisaged.
> Father, I may not understand you, but I trust you.

WEEK 2
THE MYSTERY OF SUFFERING

This week's readings centre on the book of Job, writings possibly even older than Genesis. Again we are in the realm of myth, as the first two chapters make clear, portraying goings on in heaven of which the earthly protagonists have no idea. And we are definitely in the realm of mystery, as Job, his wife and friends have no more understanding at the end than they had at the beginning, as to why his terrible sufferings came upon him. The question of why God allows suffering has been a huge issue since the earliest humans first talked around a camp fire. The logical assumption most ancient people came up with was that if someone was suffering, they must have done something to deserve it. The book of Job exists to refute that idea.

DAY 1
'Shall we receive good at the hands of the Lord and not evil?'

Read
Job 2:1–13

Understand
Job's terrible sores were the last in a multiple series of catastrophes. Raiders had taken his 500 oxen, 500 donkeys and most of his servants. Fire had destroyed his 7,000 sheep, other raiders made off with his 3,000 camels, and a tornado had killed his ten children. Nevertheless, Job understood all these as a gift from God, and so he uttered those familiar words spoken over coffins a million times since: 'The Lord has given and the Lord has taken away, blessed be the name of the Lord.' Satan reckoned that if you put someone in enough physical agony, then any faith they once had will be stripped away. But still Job in his desperation clung to his belief. Just as he had no intrinsic right to escape poverty, so, he believed, he had no right to escape pain.

Reflect
Most of us, I suspect, believe ourselves to be exempt from suffering, unless or until it comes upon us. Then we have a choice of how to react, and it is in that choice that strength of character is revealed. It is not a choice to pretend pain and loss don't exist, rather to decide that they need not alienate us from God.

Pray
Lord God, help me to accept what life throws at me,
to allow myself to weep and mourn,

but not to resent and blame,
to learn gratitude for what I've had, rather than
despair for what is lost.

DAY 2

'Miserable comforters are you all. Have windy words no limit?'

Read

Job 16:1–5 and 16:16 –17:1

Understand

Job's friends got it right the first time. To begin with they simply sat with him for seven days and nights and 'no one spoke a word to him, for they saw his suffering was too great'. It goes downhill after that. As Job pours out his grief, they feel it necessary to try and explain, and their explanation is that it must be punishment for something. 'Who that was innocent ever perished?' asked Eliphaz (4:7), a question that makes you wonder what ivory tower he'd been hiding in. Next up was Bildad who perhaps made it worse by suggesting Job's children were to blame (8:4). Zophar's unhelpful prescription was simplistic self-help: 'If you direct your heart rightly ... your life will be brighter than noonday' (11:13 and 17). No wonder Job was exasperated.

Reflect

Even had these words been true and wise, and they certainly weren't, Job was in no state to receive them. Speaking to those deep in grief is incredibly difficult. It's almost impossible to know the 'right' thing to say. But avoiding them for that reason is even worse. Our attempts to care will often be clumsy, but try we must: listening rather than speaking, finding practical helps that speak for themselves, praying, waiting – just being there.

Pray

> *Lord God, I feel so helpless in the face of others' grief.*
> *May I learn wise ways to respond,*
> *not claiming to understand when I don't.*
> *Keep me from windy words.*

DAY 3

'Where then does wisdom come from? ... It is hidden from the eyes of all living.'

Read

Job 28:20–28

Understand

It is Job who asks this question and he who answers it; in doing so, demonstrating why God felt able to put trust in him. Job realises that humans are not inherently wise. Clever, yes, knowledgeable, yes – but wise, not so much! For even the cleverest and most knowledgeable are finite, limited by time, space and brainpower in what they can know. There is only One who stands outside time and space, Job asserts, and only this One who can show the way. Wisdom comes not just from education or philosophical thinking (though these have their place), but from a very different source: a choice of humble submission to the One who knows best. Wisdom comes from willpower, not brainpower.

Reflect

Do you think you are wise? If so, beware. (And I'm aware that the very act of writing these words puts me in the danger zone!) Do you think you are weak or ignorant? If so, no problem, for acknowledging it can be a wonderful first step towards opening you up to wisdom from beyond the human sphere, brought by the Holy Spirit of God.

Pray

> *Lord God, give me a healthy mistrust of clever words.*
> *Help me to crave wisdom from a deeper source.*
> *If it comes from the deep pain of human experience,*
> *then so be it, Lord. I submit to your will.*

DAY 4

'Have you commanded the morning since your days began?'

Read

Job 38:1–12

Understand

'Were you there when I laid the foundation of the earth?' No, no one was, not even Stephen Hawking. The best his mammoth mind can do is calculate what might have been. Have you ever made the sun rise? No, no one has, not Copernicus, not Newton, not Einstein. The best these scientific geniuses could do is try to understand how it happened. True, humans have learned how to make light appear at the flick of a switch, to unlock energy sources from the earth's crust, or harness the power of winds and waves. But even these giant leaps are only utilising what was already there, waiting for us to discover. All these achievements show that God designed us with amazing capabilities, but remind us that even the most brilliant of us cannot create life[2] or matter out of nothing.

Reflect

Here is a simple practical suggestion. One day this week get up a little earlier to allow time to sit and watch the dawn. You may not catch an actual sunrise, but even so, watch with wonder the way light returns and colour seeps back into the greyness. Perhaps you'll notice the singing stars or the swaddling clouds, the rain, or the hoar frost. Be amazed.

Pray

> *Lord God, shake me loose from what I take for granted.*
> *Prise me free from dull self-absorption.*
> *Give me child-like wonder*
> *and open my eyes to marvels I'd forgotten.*

DAY 5

'I have uttered what I did not understand, things too wonderful for me ...'

Read

Job 42:1–10

Understand

In the face of God's thunderous questioning, there is only one response. Job needs to shut up. His understanding has been radically altered. 'I had heard of you by the hearing of the ear, but now my eye sees you.' Experiencing something you had only been told about before – childbirth, the Grand Canyon, love, pain, death – changes your perception forever. And no experience changes you more deeply than an encounter with the living Creator God. It happens to a few in great dramatic intensity, to most as a fleeting moment barely understood, but it can throw into question all you thought you knew. The story of Job concludes with a happy ending. Job's fortunes were fully restored, even his friends' folly was forgiven. I'm sure, however, that none of them were ever quite the same. What, I wonder, was the difference?

Reflect

How can you ensure you do not speak things you don't understand? Here are some suggestions. Listen more and speak less. Listen to what you say, listen out for platitudes, sweeping generalities, jargon that has solidified into habit. Identify those things you need to understand more. Learn to say 'I don't know' and 'I was wrong'. Learn to laugh at your absurdities.

Pray

Lord God, keep me from foolish words.
May I not rush to fill a holy silence.
May I look and listen carefully and acknowledge my
*   mistakes.*
May I sit humbly, prayerfully and patiently with those
*   who suffer.*

WEEK 3
THE MYSTERY OF GOD'S CARE

This week we move away from myth and into the realm of poetry. The Psalms were written with patterns and rhythms now lost in translation. For example, they often use a technique of echoing one thought with a similar one, as in Psalm 119:105: '... a lamp to my feet and a light to my path'. But they are more than exercises in beautiful language. Many are prayers, addressed directly to God. Others are calls to prayer, reminding the hearer of God's power and love. All are written to be used in worship. But above all they are cries from the depths of human emotion: joy, guilt, despair, fear, anger. They are deeply honest and affirm that there is no feeling or experience we cannot bring to God and nowhere his care will not reach.

DAY 1
'What are human beings ... that you care for them?'

Read
Psalm 8

Understand
Last week I suggested you took time to watch a sunrise. This week perhaps you should take a moment to stare into the (hopefully unclouded) night sky. That is what the psalmist had been doing, provoking a question every human down the ages has asked: 'Who am I in all this?' Of course the very fact the question is being asked points

to the answer. Humans are the only creatures with the consciousness, intelligence and drive to wonder why. But the psalmist was asking more than 'What are we?' His question was: 'What are we *that you are mindful of us, that you care for us?*' It is an awareness that out of all creation not only are humans special in their unique attributes, but because the Creator cares directly for them.

Reflect

How did the Bible writers come to understand that every person on earth was held in the mind of God? And how come so many now doubt it? After all, computers have now shown us how detailed information on millions of us can be held and accessed simultaneously. The mind of God must be not only vastly more powerful than any computer, but more personal, imbued with perfect love.

Pray

 Lord God, how amazing that you hold me and my
  doings in your mind.
 How wonderful that this is not dispassionate
  knowledge, but suffused with passionate love.
 Thank you, Lord, I do not deserve it.

DAY 2

'Why are you cast down, O my soul, and why are you disquieted within me?'

Read

Psalm 42

Ponder

'Why do I feel like this? What is this angst eating away at me?' I can count my blessings, keep a smile on my face, even talk the God-talk, but inside I feel dry, empty and desperate. In the last passage, the psalmist took a leap of faith that God was 'mindful' of humans. In this passage the writer feels forgotten. Has God changed or is it the individual? The voice of faith tells us God does not change. Nevertheless, experience tells us there are times when God apparently withdraws – sometimes when we need him most. The psalmist does not get an answer. He can only reiterate the hope that restoration will come. What this psalm does suggest though is that there is nothing blameworthy, or even unusual, about feeling depressed. Faith is not about being on a permanent high. It's about trusting through the lows as well.

Reflect

It is a harsh reality that when we ask 'Why me? Why now?' explanations may not be forthcoming. What evidence does show is that it's often through the lows rather than the highs that character is grown. Could God be hiding himself for a reason? Is it a sign of his trust in us?

Pray

Lord God, sometimes I feel dry, empty and desperate,
and it seems unreasonable that things should be so.
I accept that I may never know the reason.
But work in me through the dryness, Lord, I pray.

DAY 3
'Wash me and I shall be whiter than snow.'

Read
Psalm 51:1–12

Understand

Many psalms are attributed to the Jewish king, David. This one relates directly to an incident where he quite spectacularly screwed up. It's found in 2 Samuel 11 and 12 and it's a cynical blend of adultery, deception and murder. Only one brave man, the prophet Nathan, was prepared to confront the king with his crime. Amazingly, he got away with it; the result could have been Nathan's execution, but in fact it was David's acknowledgement of guilt. Even more amazingly, David 'got away with it' before God. There *were* consequences, terrible ones of family conflict and dysfunctional leadership, but he could be forgiven. Can anyone then be forgiven? we ask, shocked. The astonishing answer this psalm gives is that, yes, God's forgiveness is possible even for the darkest wrongdoing.

Reflect

The depression described in yesterday's passage had no known reason, but sometimes we all know there is a cause: guilt, imagined or all too real. Either way, the stain can be washed away. A 'new and right spirit' can replace the dirty, weary old one. This cleansing doesn't come lightly, for God or for us. For God it took the greatest possible sacrifice of love, for us a 'broken spirit' (v17) is the key.

Pray

Lord God, so often I don't feel right with myself.
My sins may not be spectacular King David ones,
but they niggle and itch and stain and spoil.
You know them, Lord. Please make me clean again.

DAY 4
'How weighty to me are your thoughts, O God!'

Read
Psalm 139:1–10 and 16–18

Ponder
The idea that all our ways are recorded in the database that is God's mind is both awesome and deeply disturbing. We don't want anyone to know the unvarnished truth about ourselves, certainly not God. Even more mind-blowing than the idea that it's all down there in God's 'book' is that it was there even before we existed. 'Before' is the wrong

word, of course, because God is outside time. (If there's no 'before', then there's no *pre*-destination, of course, so free will stands unchallenged.) It's not just factual information, the psalm suggests, but 'thoughts' that have been 'sifted' (the literal meaning of 'searched'), so motives or actions or contributing circumstances that we would struggle to untangle, understand or remember are all known.

Reflect
Wherever you are, God is there. It's a scary thought, especially if you're carrying guilt you choose not to admit. It may seem possible to hide, but it's an illusion, rather like the child who thinks if they put a blanket over their head, they become invisible. But if you want help, and aren't too proud to admit it, then the knowledge that God understands all about you and is always close at hand can be profoundly comforting.

Pray
Lord God, help me to stand beneath your searching gaze and not be afraid of what you might see.
If I need to know it, then reveal it, Lord.
I trust your understanding – so much better than mine.

DAY 5
'He determines the number of the stars.'

Read
Psalm 147:1–11

Understand
Cosmologists spend whole careers trying to 'determine the number of the stars' and they've made great strides – though it sometimes seems the more they discover, the more they find undiscovered beyond. There's an intriguing juxtaposition in this psalm: a God who not only knows the whole universe, but knows each person whose heart

is breaking. And not just knows the ailment, or prescribes the cure, but actually comes down to us, to apply the ointment and dress the wound. This understanding of the immensely large and the incredibly small is 'beyond measure', says the psalmist. In other words, God's understanding is way beyond the power of science. Even if physicists do find a 'theory of everything', they really won't have discovered the mind of God!

Reflect

How much attention do we give to the broken-hearted? The smashed self-esteem of a jilted teenager, the crushed dignity of a redundant worker, the lost identity of a stateless refugee, the fractured mind of an Alzheimer's victim – how often do we turn away, hoping they will somehow 'get over it' or ' learn to cope'? God gets close, weeping alongside, offering hope. Mustn't he long for us to do the same?

Pray

Lord God, we may never understand the stars like a
*   cosmologist,*
*   but we can learn more of the broken hearts*
*   around us.*
May we grasp just a little bit of your understanding
*   of those we meet,*
*   and may our hands be used to bind their wounds.*

WEEK 4
THE MYSTERY OF WISDOM

We move on this week to the books of the Bible known as wisdom literature. Unlike Psalms whose natural habitat is the place of worship, these books are for home and workplace, Proverbs asking the question 'how?' do we live, and Ecclesiastes asking 'why?'

Proverbs is the gathered writings of several authors, a higgledy-piggledy collection of pithy sayings on everyday matters such as friendship, parenting, business dealings and marriage. Much could be described as common sense, but it returns again and again to a very much deeper wisdom.

Ecclesiastes is the product of one writer – and a less ecclesiastical one would be hard to find. This is a world-weary philosopher, with a familiar sceptical catchphrase: 'Vanity of vanities, all is vanities.' In other words, everything is futile! But despite his cynicism, he too turns to a deeper wisdom in the end.

DAY 1
'Cry out for insight ... for wisdom will come into your heart.'

Read
Proverbs 2:1–15

Understand
The speaker is a father addressing a child, urgently trying to instil an understanding of true wisdom. This wisdom comes from two sources: teaching handed down through the generations and direct revelation from God. Both these sources are precious, to be searched out, dug into, mined like silver. This is not head knowledge, but heart knowledge, not rote learning but deep insight. This is about far more than handy information – just look at all those words describing a good way of life: uprightness, blamelessness, faithfulness, righteousness, justice, equity (fairness) and prudence. This sort of knowledge, once deep inside you, fully infusing who you are, will act as a safeguard, making you no longer vulnerable either to your own destructive urges or to the cruelty or deviousness of others.

Reflect
'The longest journey', it has been said, 'is the journey from your head to your heart.'[3] It is extremely easy to hear something wise, moderately easy to comprehend it

and not too difficult to remember it; but to take it right
inside yourself so that you live it out – that is a different
story. It takes effort, willingness and time, quite probably
a lifetime. Is it a quest you are still engaged on?

Pray

> *Lord God, rekindle in me an urgency,*
> *a determination to gain true wisdom,*
> *to take it down to the deepest parts of my being,*
> *so it may become part of who I am.*

DAY 2
'She is a tree of life to those who lay hold of her ...'

Read

Proverbs 3:1–18

Ponder

The wisdom described in yesterday's and today's
passages is hard won. It requires trust; relying on insights
that might not always seem wise 'in your own eyes'. It
also involves correction, described as coming from the
Lord, but in practice, as we all know, most often through
the school of hard knocks. There is trust involved here
too, trust that God is working within it: speaking his
wisdom through the harsh words of others, redeeming
and reworking failure and mistakes. But what this hard
schooling brings, says the writer, is serenity. The sort of
happiness described here is deeper than mere enjoyment.
It is 'abundant welfare', life that, whether or not long in
measured time, is full to the brim in experienced time.

Reflect

Can you think of anyone who seems to have 'won
through' tough times into a serenity you envy? This
passage tells you this serenity is there for you too. It is

a way of life that can be gained by anyone, precisely
because it does not come from your own wisdom,
but from trusting in a power beyond. All it requires is
humility, grateful honouring and a willingness to learn.

Pray

Lord God, help me to trust more in you than in me.
Help me to honour you as the source of my well-being.
Help me to listen to those who might see my flaws
* better than I can.*
and help me to believe this deeper wisdom can live
* even in me.*

DAY 3
'I was beside him like a master worker ... delighting in
the human race.'

Read
Proverbs 8:22–31

Ponder
Here we have Wisdom revealed for who she is, none
other than the Holy Spirit, the third person of the
Godhead along with Christ. (You will have noticed by
now that Wisdom in these passages is referred to as
female, which seems appropriate, both in redressing the
gender imbalance, and because the Holy Spirit often
works in those ways we describe as feminine: intuitive,
encouraging, gentle.) But what is amazing about this
passage is that it describes that gentle, encouraging,
intuitive presence as working *with* God, *before* the
beginning, outside the limitations of time. She is revealed
as a master craftsperson, actively involved in God's
creative work. And what is so striking is how much they
are enjoying it! Not only is there mutual delight between
them, but delight in the world they are making, and most
especially in the human race.

Reflect

This passage gives an understanding of our origins quite different from evolution or the Big Bang. Working with the human race is a presence from beyond time, entirely concerned with how you conduct yourself: with practical things like justice and equity and prudence, as well as with spiritual attitudes.

Pray

Lord God: Father, Son and Holy Spirit,
may I delight in you, as you delight in me.
May I listen to Wisdom from outside the bounds of time,
and put it into practice in the minutiae of daily life.

DAY 4

'A capable wife ... is far more precious than jewels.'

Read

Proverbs 31:10–20 and 25–30

Understand

It didn't seem right to leave Proverbs, especially in the context of our movie, without looking at this poem of praise for a good woman. The old saying that behind every successful man is a good woman must be broadened somewhat these days, but it is still true that behind those who succeed in the public sphere there is usually a behind-the-scenes person: a homemaker, a personal assistant, a carer. And very rarely do these behind-the-scenes people get the credit they deserve. In a world of ready meals, labour-saving devices and online shopping, this is particularly true of homemaking. For true homemaking is far more than practical stuff. It involves creating an environment where the natural world is cared for, where beauty is valued, where all are welcomed and appreciated, and where the attributes of wisdom are demonstrated daily.

Reflect

Each one of us comes from and returns to a home. It need be little more than refrigerator, microwave, TV, bed, sofa and shower, but if that is all home means then our society will be deeply impoverished. If we are to enrich our world, then our homes need to be places where hospitality is practised, where neighbours are greeted and looked out for, where family is valued; and not least sacred spaces, where God is met and listened to.

Pray

Lord God, may I value those behind-the-scenes
*   people in my life.*
If my role is hidden, then may I understand its worth.
Make my home a place where you are welcome,
and where others are valued too.

DAY 5
'He has made everything beautiful in its time.'[4]

Read

Ecclesiastes 3:1–15

Understand

A recurring theme of this course is that of time: its limitations, its uncertainty, its relentlessness. For each of us, life has a rhythm, that of our individual lives and that of history; sometimes we can choose that rhythm, but often we cannot. (Most readers of this book will be remarkable in having lived entirely in a time of peace and plenty.) But whatever we live through, concludes Ecclesiastes, 'everything is beautiful in its time'. It is possible for people to be happy, to do good, to eat and drink and find satisfaction in their work. And time is not all there is. God has 'set eternity' in our hearts. We sense that there is more: that 'everything God does will endure'.

Reflect

What season of life are you in right now? Planting or plucking, mourning or laughing, keeping or discarding? Whatever it is, can you find a sense of beauty, or rightness within it? There's an old poem which pictures life as a woven tapestry, but one only seen from the back. All we know are the loose ends, the random threads; there seems to be no picture. 'Not till the loom is silent, and the shuttles cease to fly, shall God unroll the canvas, and explain the reason why.' We cannot fathom, but God can.

Pray

> Lord God, my times are in your hand.
> Help me to accept and to savour this season of my life,
> help me to find beauty within it,
> to enjoy life and do good.

WEEK 5
THE MYSTERY OF WEAKNESS

We move on now to the writings of Paul, encircling the heart of the Bible, the Gospels, in order finally to return there in the run-up to Easter. Paul's writings are often convoluted and sometimes obscure, though each passage contains amazing nuggets of revelation. Paul reads like a man who once thought he had his certainties all in place until suddenly they were turned upside down. That, of course, is exactly what happened to him, as his religious assumptions were challenged by Jesus, the man he once dismissed as a heretic. So, far from being works of considered doctrine, these are letters from someone for whom this is all new. Paul is working out his understanding as he goes along, and it sometimes reads that way; nevertheless, his genius and deep understanding should never be underestimated.

DAY 1

'But God chose what is weak in the world to shame the strong.'

Read
1 Corinthians 1:20–31

Understand
Paul must have felt very vulnerable. He had once been an up-and-coming member of the Jewish establishment. Now he was an outsider, trying to communicate with others who rejected his message for entirely different reasons. For the Greeks it wasn't logical enough, for the Jews not miraculous enough. It didn't arise from respectable knowledge and learning, it didn't manifest itself in respectable power structures. Even worse, it wasn't the elite from these rival establishments who were joining the new movement, rather a rag-bag of people from who knows where. But because Paul understood that it was a religion birthed in the ultimate weakness of Christ on the cross, he grasped too that weakness was to be its strength. Because it was only in that weakness that the new believers would reach out for the strength that came from God.

Reflect
Do you feel vulnerable as a follower of Christ in a sceptical world? Do you feel unable to explain your faith? Do you feel you're not strong enough or smart enough to carry out the tasks before you? Good, says Paul, because that is why God chose you. And because he chose you, his strength will carry you through.

Pray
*Lord God, some mornings I don't feel strong enough
    for the day ahead.
Some evenings I feel I've failed at even the most basic
    tasks.*

Sometimes I realise I got things quite wrong.
Lord, come to me in my weakness, I pray.

DAY 2
'... so that what is mortal may be swallowed up by life.'

Read
2 Corinthians 4:16–5:10

Understand
What Paul is talking about here is the frailty of the human body, using the metaphor of a tent. What our human spirits are clothed in now is a conglomerate of bone and muscle, blood and brains, wonderful in its construction, but vulnerable to being blown away by the merest alien microbe. But, says Paul, this earthly body is only temporary, there is another secure, strong, permanent home that awaits us. Paul's confidence cannot be proven, but has a strong rationale. Paul knew that everything in the material world was bounded by time and prone to decay. But what he also 'knew' by revelation and faith was that those 'unseen' and unquantifiable values – love, beauty, hope, glory – are eternal. These are what constitute true life, and one day the pale version of it that we now live will be 'swallowed up' into something bigger and far more wonderful.

Reflect
If you believe this life is all there is, then fear of losing physical existence can become all-consuming. But if this life is only a temporary stopover en route to somewhere more permanent, then the perspective changes. It does not make physical decay any easier, but it perhaps makes it more bearable.

Pray
Lord God, I see my elder loved ones declining and
fading away.

I feel my own body's vulnerability to pains and strains.
Give me a new perspective, Lord.
Help me glimpse a beyond in which all this will be
    forgotten.

DAY 3

'My grace is sufficient for you, for power is made
perfect in weakness.'

Read
2 Corinthians 12:1–10

Understand
Paul comes across as something of a conflicted character
in this passage. 'I want to boast, but I won't boast, and if
I am boasting what of it, but I'm not really ...' Boy, this
guy is confused! Then there's the strange bit about this
'person', who it turns out must be Paul himself, with
his amazing experience of 'being caught up to Paradise'.
And then there is that 'thorn in the flesh'. Was it
physical pain, mental weakness, sexual temptation? No
one knows. But whatever it was, it served an essential
purpose. This passage clearly demonstrates how conceit
could have been Paul's downfall. As it is, his weakness
became what made him – someone who discovered over
and over that God's grace was all he needed.

Reflect
Look at the Church down the ages, and you will see an
establishment (or more accurately, several rival ones)
constantly seeking power and control, for the Church,
like all human institutions, is prey to human self-
seeking. But look at those individual Christians who
inspire you: Julian of Norwich, John Wesley, Mother
Teresa, Pope Francis. You see something very different:
people who've discovered that following Jesus means
giving up self in favour of weakness and grace.

Pray

Lord God, I admit I am full of inner conflict.
I can be conceited (in a subtle self-deprecating way,
*   of course),*
*   self-seeking and infuriated by my own weaknesses.*
Please take all that away, Lord, and replace it with
*   your grace.*

DAY 4
'I have learned to be content with whatever I have.'

Read
Philippians 4:4–13

Understand
This reads like an older and wiser Paul, who through the long hard road of experience has discovered a gracious acceptance. The key to his contentment can be found in those 'always' and 'everything' statements. 'Rejoice in the Lord *always* ... Do not worry about *anything* ... In *everything*, let your requests be known to God... I can do *all things* through Christ who strengthens me.' This is the credo of someone who over long years has learned not to try pulling himself up by his own bootstraps, but to hand everything over to the wisdom of a higher power. Paul began with a hypothesis, that the power of Christ could supply the grace he needed for a risky lifestyle with the normal props taken away. And as he experimented, in all extremes of circumstances, he found it to be true.

Reflect
Contentment does not come automatically with age, success or comfortable circumstances. It rarely comes suddenly when bidden. Rather it is a habit of mind that must be learned. There is a certain 'power of positive thinking' involved, looking for what is good in every circumstance and every person. But mind tricks can

only go so far. When these things fail, it is 'him who strengthens me' to whom we must turn.

Pray

> *Lord God, help me to cultivate habits of seeing.*
> *Show me the good that is there for me in every*
> *   circumstance.*
> *But beyond that, when it seems nothing I see is right*
> *   or good,*
> *then help me to cultivate habits of trusting.*

DAY 5

'... the riches of the glory of this mystery, which is Christ in you.'

Read

Colossians 1:24–2:7

Understand

When it comes to the mystery of everything, Paul believes he has found the key – it is Jesus Christ. He speaks of what he's found in terms of great value: 'riches', 'glory' and 'treasures', and as something once hidden and now revealed. Yet in this passage, Paul seems to be struggling, indeed it's a word he repeats here, to communicate what he's discovered. Paul was proud to be Jewish. He knew his Scriptures and realised that the great gifts those writings described – God's compassion and wisdom – were somehow now embodied in Jesus. He realised too that they were gifts that transcended nation and birth. But when it came to explaining the why and how – not so easy!

Reflect

Perhaps what we should take from this passage is that faith really isn't easy to explain. It really has to be experienced – by those who are rooted in a commitment to follow Christ's Way. So perhaps we shouldn't beat ourselves up when we find it so hard to explain what we believe, rather accept that we are in the presence of mystery, and rejoice that our faith rests not on a 'what' to be understood, but a 'who' to be followed.

Pray

Lord God, there is so much I can't understand,
and much that I can grasp deep inside, but can't
explain in words.
Help me to simply trust your Spirit of Wisdom
and simply follow your Son Jesus Christ.

HOLY WEEK
THE MYSTERY OF THE CROSS

It seemed appropriate to bring this Bible reading exercise to completion, by ending on what for Christians must be the heart of it all, the life of Jesus Christ. The purpose of Lent is to lead up to Easter and the mystery of Jesus' death and resurrection. In these readings, though, we will not be looking at the actual accounts of those events, as you will probably hear these at church services. Rather we look here at what Jesus himself said about them, before and afterwards, and what he understood was happening.

DAY 1

'Those who want to lose their life for my sake will save it.'

Read
Luke 9:18–25

Ponder
When Jesus asks who the disciples think he is, Peter is certain: he is the Messiah, the 'Chosen One', who it was believed would come one day to herald in a new kingdom of justice. Jesus accepts the title but does not

want it used. He explains what he expects to happen, that he will be killed and then raised. And then he makes this extraordinary statement that his followers must take up their cross. He qualifies it with this curious word: 'daily', so he is clearly not advocating martyrdom as a lifestyle. What he is saying is that the kingdom he has come to usher in is quite paradoxical. It has much to do with self-denial and little to do with power.

Reflect

What does it mean to you to take up your cross daily? It must mean, I think, something about living in this topsy-turvy kingdom, with values quite different from the world's. It must also mean something about accepting those sufferings and difficulties which come to us, and sharing the burdens of those that come to others. It is about giving rather than gaining, about letting go of self, rather than clinging on.

Pray

> *Lord God, being a follower of yours was never going to be easy.*
> *At times it seems way too hard for me.*
> *Self-seeking isn't going to work, you say, self-giving is.*
> *I do believe you. So help me try to follow where you lead.*

DAY 2
'This is my body which is given for you.'

Read

Luke 22:14–27

Ponder

As he often does, Jesus implies something astonishing here, rather than fully explaining it. That's why the context is so important. The meal being celebrated is the Passover, a ritual that draws on the idea of animal sacrifice, generally understood by ancient peoples as a way of appeasing God for wrongdoing. In this instance it celebrates the Jewish escape from Egyptian slavery, when the sacrifice of a lamb was the sign that brought them freedom. So when Jesus lifts the bread and the cup he is drawing on this deep understanding of sacrifice as a route to both forgiveness and freedom. There is a purely circumstantial explanation for his forthcoming death: the Jewish authorities want to bring him down. But, Jesus implies, there is something far deeper going on as well.

Reflect
The words of this passage may be familiar to you from the communion service, expressing the central Christian understanding that Jesus' death acts as a sacrifice for all who trust him, that his brokenness can restore us to wholeness. This is a mystery, the 'how' and 'why' of which is beyond most of us ordinary believers. But it is not blind faith, rather it is based on the experience that this makes all the difference.

Pray
> Lord God, the deep meaning embodied in the bread
>   and wine
> brings nourishment to my spirit and for this I thank
>   you.
> Let this never be to me ritual for the sake of it,
>   but something that impacts and changes the
>   whole of my being.

DAY 3
'In a little while the world will no longer see me, but you will see me ...'

Read
John 14:15–27

Understand

Jesus is gradually explaining more to his followers, and here he tells them that he must now leave, but that his physical absence will make way for a new presence, that of the Holy Spirit. We may well make the link with the Spirit of Wisdom described in Proverbs, the same Spirit who was with God before the creation of the universe. Now, Jesus says, that Spirit is available in a new and more intimate way. He describes this presence as a Counsellor, one who teaches and advises. The word, though, can be translated Advocate, implying someone who represents our case before God – in other words, a two-way go-between. Jesus makes it clear this new presence is for all who are committed to following his way, and that they will see him after his death.

Reflect

In this passage, Jesus puts your relationship with God on a whole new footing. God is no longer the distant Almighty, but Father, so you can be 'family' with God, Jesus and Holy Spirit. 'We will make our home with them,' says Jesus, and 'them', if you are a follower of Jesus, means you too.

Pray

Lord God – or Father, for through Jesus I can call
you that.
Thank you that you can be 'at home' in me
And I can receive wisdom from you.
Please keep that relationship alive in me.
Lord, I welcome you.

DAY 4

'This is my commandment, that you love one another.'

Read

John 15:9–17

Understand

To me this is the heart of the heart of things. The heart of the Bible is Jesus and the heart of Jesus' message is this simple command: Love one another. This love is more than affection or companionship, this is that strong, gritty *agape* love that cares for the other through thick and thin. It is the ultimate expression of this love, says Jesus, that is about to be enacted in his death, in the laying down of his life for his friends. The words were spoken specifically to his companions in that room, but they soon realised they were for all who followed. It happened shortly afterwards, when the Holy Spirit came dramatically to all races and all sorts of people, that this truth became undeniably obvious.

Reflect

If we accept this understanding that God is love, what a difference it makes. It takes away all the old understandings of God as remote and implacable. Basically, God need no longer be scary. It took Jesus and his death to dispel those old understandings once and for all, and to show that this was a servant leadership, a Father God, a kingdom of love not power.

Pray

Lord God, sometimes that residual fear resurfaces in me,
that you must be a tyrant and not a kind friend,
that guilt must be a more appropriate response than joy.
Help me to understand what it means to live in a
*   kingdom of love.*

DAY 5

'Blessed are those who have not seen and yet have come to believe.'

Read
John 20:19–29

Ponder

Jesus had predicted he would rise from death and that his followers would see him. And despite their evident disbelief, they did. But poor old Thomas had been missing from that first great moment, and Thomas was a true scientist (though the term would not be invented for another 1,800 years[6]). He was not prepared to go on hearsay, he wanted evidence – and evidence was what he got. Earlier in this course we asked the question, 'Does God ever break the natural laws he himself put in place?' The resurrection makes the Christian position unequivocal – yes, he can and he does, if he has reason to. And this was the most important reason ever, that all might believe and receive new life for themselves.

Reflect

Jesus did not condemn Thomas's doubt. Rather he pointed out that tangible evidence was relatively easy; spiritual evidence is very much harder. But spiritual evidence is available to us. We can all consider what is lovely and what is ugly, what brings peace and what brings discontent, what is right and what is wrong. It is this evidence we must evaluate as we decide whether to trust in the risen Christ – and then take a leap of faith!

Pray

Lord God, I don't find believing in miracles easy,
so I'm glad you didn't condemn 'doubting' Thomas.
Help me to trust those things that are certainties in my
*   spiritual experience,*
and live at peace with those that are mystery.

LEADER'S NOTES

TRUST THE PROCESS

This course is particularly open-ended, with diverse questions and often without obvious conclusions. Taken all together, though, there is a pattern and learning outcomes will evolve. If necessary, reassure participants to trust the process. Encourage them to commit time to the Bible readings and background chapters, as these will fill in a great deal that is not covered in the sessions.

This course is also unusual in that it discusses the story of real-life people. Some background information on the real story is given in these notes. Use your discretion as to whether to share it, and ensure that people speak of the story's protagonists with respect and compassion.

PREPARE THE PRACTICALITIES

FILM CLIPS

Before the session starts make sure that the disc is set up ready on the appropriate chapter on the menu. Please make sure you know the idiosyncrasies of your DVD player. If you leave the film on pause, ensure that the player will not automatically drop out of this after a short time, allowing the TV to come crashing in! All clips begin at the start of a chapter, and on only one session is there more than one clip – in this case, go back to the menu at the end of the first clip and set up for the next one. Review the film first and ensure you know the 'out cue'.

QUESTIONS

There are four different types of question in this course. It may be a good idea to explain these differences as you go through Session 1. The suggested differences are as follows:

Ask

A more straightforward question that does not necessarily lead to discussion, and may or may not provoke personal anecdote.

Discuss

More controversial ideas or complex subjects that may require some debate.

Brainstorm

Short quick-fire answers. It may be worth writing the answers up on a sheet or board.

Ponder and share

Sharing of personal experiences which may take some time to recall, so allow a short time of quiet first (30 seconds to 1 minute) for people to think. This is not the place for discussion.

MEDITATION

Before the meditation starts, organise different people to read the different sections.

SILENCE OR MUSIC

Some people feel uncomfortable with silence and prefer background music for quiet thought, while others hate it. It may be wise to ring the changes and also seek out opinions. If you do use music, find something gentle and unobtrusive, probably instrumental. (The music of Margaret Rizza is ideal for this purpose.) Ensure it is ready to play in instantly and someone can do it from where they are sitting; that they have a watch or have planned the length beforehand, and that it is faded out rather than abruptly cut.

BIBLE READINGS

Think about what version you want to use, and provide it, ready with marker in place. In some cases a contemporary version like *The Message* may give the passage a fresh slant. You can find all versions on www.biblegateway.com. Print them out beforehand if necessary.

SESSION 1

Show film clip: Chapters 3 and 4

IN:　　10 mins 2 secs　　　Knock on the door 'Come in'
OUT:　19 mins 10 secs　　After Jane sees box of Tide
　　　　　　　　　　　　　on the doorstep

Brainstorm

What did you see that showed how Stephen and Jane experience awe and wonder and delight?

- Falling in love
- Poetry – quotes W. B. Yeats, says she likes William Blake
- Art – Turner
- Scientific discovery
- Atoms: the tiniest building blocks of life
- Stars: the vastness of the universe
- UV light
- Beauty – the magical environment of Cambridge and the May Ball
- Music and dancing
- Church and the Bible.

SESSION 2

NB This evening's meditation uses one large candle and enough tea-lights for everyone so please ensure that you have these, plus matches and/or taper set out ready before the whole session begins!

You may find that the Bible reading from 2 Corinthians works better from a contemporary version: *The Message* is a good one here. Take time to find it and print out ready to use if necessary.

Show film clip: Chapters 7 and 8   *12 mins*
In: 34 mins 53 secs   Stephen to Schiama
Out: 47 mins 28 secs   After 'I've had an idea'

Brainstorm
List all the ways – from the big scientific picture to our daily lives in which our experience of time is mysterious.

Big picture:
- Vast ages of the earth before humans came on the scene
- Relativity: spacetime continuum
- Time at the level of quantum physics.

Daily lives:
- Can only experience it forwards
- Never seem to have enough time
- Some moments seem very long, others pass in an instant
- We have no idea of our own time span.

Ask
Jane is determined to fight Stephen's illness. What weapons does she have?
- Love, determination, faith in God and in Stephen.

Brainstorm
List the emotions we see in Stephen, Jane and their friends as his illness progresses.

Stephen:
- Frustration, envy of others with no problems, pride, denial, despair, determination, perseverance, intuition.

Jane:
- Patience, compassion, struggling to keep a brave face.

Friends:
- Humour, awkwardness, uncertainty.

Supplementary questions
Sharing experiences of suffering and of being a carer are likely to vary in length depending on how many people in the group have such experiences. Don't rush these sharing sessions, but if they do prove short, these extra questions could be slotted in.

Meditation
If possible, dim the lights (allowing enough for readers!) and light just one candle on a central table. Put out enough tea-lights for each participant. Ensure that they can light them from the central candle or that a taper or lighter is available.

SESSION 3
Show film clip: Chapter 11 and part Chapter 12 *10 mins*
IN: 58 mins 43 secs   Jane goes into church
OUT: 1 hour 09 mins   Jane and Stephen in bed, as music stops

Discuss
Is Jane and Jonathan's developing relationship right or wrong?

We will be missing out the part of the film where Jane

tells Jonathan that she is pregnant. It is clear from his reaction that he knows he could not be the father. She also insists to his parents that the child is Stephen's. This bears out all biographical information, from Stephen and from Jane.

We will also skip the later point where Jane and Jonathan are camping, and it is implied that the relationship is now consummated. Jane's book makes clear that at some point it did develop into a sexual relationship, with what she understood as Stephen's tacit approval. Jane's book says that at some point in the 1980s they 'allowed the relationship to blossom', but that they observed a strict code of conduct, keeping the relationship strictly on a friendship level in front of Stephen, the children and others, and that they were alone together very rarely. She notes that these rare moments of intimacy 'paradoxically reinforced our loyalty to Stephen'.[1]

Show film clip: Chapter 14

| IN: | 1 hour 21 mins | Stephen in intensive care |
| OUT: | 1 hour 24 mins 23 secs | Trees blowing seen from window |

Discuss

How do we as Christians react to relationships that are outside the traditional norms?

In her book, Jane notes that she and Jonathan did go to the vicar of the church they attended for guidance and that he helped to 'strengthen our resolve and help keep our perspective within the disciplined framework'. Clearly he reacted with compassion and expressed his understanding that their situation was unique. She also notes that Don Page, one of Stephen's scientific collaborators and a strong evangelical Christian with 'absolute values', conceded how incredibly demanding living with Stephen could be and how dealing with it challenged his own conscience.[2]

SESSION 4

Show film clip: Chapters 16 and 17

IN: 1 hr 31 mins   Stephen sitting in room
                             (before 'Daisy, Daisy')

OUT: 1 hr 41 mins 32 secs   After removal men
                             packing up, Jane stands
                             alone, music draws to
                             close *before* Christmas
                             choir)

Summary of session

This may be the point at which to bring in some background information on the real-life situation.

In reality Elaine was just one of a team of nurses brought in to care for Stephen after his tracheotomy. (The tracheotomy tube had to be cleaned regularly, a specialist task that required 24-hour professional attention.) A philanthropic organisation in the USA gave a large grant to cover this. Although in some ways this eased Jane's problems, in other ways this situation made things even more difficult. She had the job of recruiting and managing a team of nurses, not all of whom turned out to be suitable. The family home was now invaded at all times by strangers, some of whom were not backward in voicing their opinions. Elaine, in particular, was critical of the few hours teaching Jane now did per week, and suggested that she ought to train as a nurse and devote herself to Stephen.

Perhaps the film reference to *Penthouse* magazine needs to be explained. Stephen had a bet with one of his fellow physicists, Kip Thorne, that a star thought to have a companion black hole did not indeed have one. In fact

Stephen believed the black hole did exist, the bet was a kind of consolation in case of his work being wasted. If Stephen won, Kip Thorne would buy him a subscription to *Private Eye*. If Thorne won, Hawking would get him a subscription to *Penthouse*. In 1990 Hawking lost the bet – that is, his prediction turned out to be correct![3]

Incidentally, the engineer who set up the voice synthesiser was Elaine Mason's husband David.

SESSION 5

Beforehand make sure that, if wished, you have a copy of the Colossians reading in *The Message* translation (NB: in this translation it starts more conveniently from v26).

Ask
What different types of love did you see in the relationships between the characters in the film, and when did one sort of love spill over into another?

Jane and Stephen's love began as Eros and Friendship, but the long years of Jane's caring for Stephen turned it, by Jane's own admission, into a mother–child Affection relationship.

Jane and Jonathan's relationship began as Friendship before tipping over into Eros love.

Jane and Stephen (and Jonathan) displayed parental Affection for the children.

Stephen and Elaine's relationship began with Eros love.

Both Jane and Jonathan displayed immense amounts of *Agape* love towards Stephen.

All

The Grace

Think about what might work for your group, and if it is frequently used in your context, try and make it a little different.

If you normally look round at each other while you say it, why not suggest that you look round at each other *before* you say it, mentally acknowledging each person in the room.

If you normally hold hands as you say it, then don't, acknowledging each person in their individuality and uniqueness. If you never hold hands, then now might be a good moment to do so.

REFERENCES

All Bible references are from the New Revised Standard Version, unless otherwise stated.

INTRODUCTION
1 *The Theory of Everything*, Director: James Marsh, Screenplay: Anthony McCarten, Universal Studios, 2014.
2 René Descartes quoted by Paul Ricoeur.
3 Paul Ricoeur, *Fallible Man*, Fordham University Press, 1965.
4 Johnny Nash, 'There are more questions than answers', 1972.
5 M. Scott Peck, *Further Along the Road Less Travelled*, Simon and Schuster, 1993.
6 Stephen Hawking, *A Brief History of Time*, Bantam, 1988.
7 Jane Hawking, *Travelling to Infinity: My Life with Stephen*, Alma Books, 2007.

WEEK 1
Opening quotes:
    Annie Dillard, *Pilgrim at Tinker Creek*, Canterbury Press, 1974.
    Albert Einstein, *Science, Philosophy and Religion: A Symposium*, New York, 1941.
1 Stephen Hawking, *A Brief History of Time*.
2 William Wordsworth, 'Lines Composed a Few Miles above Tintern Abbey', 1798.
3 William Blake, 'Auguries of Innocence', 1803.
4 C. S. Lewis, *Surprised by Joy*, Geoffrey Bles, 1955.
5 Stephen Hawking, interview in *New Scientist*, quoted in *The Telegraph*, 4 January 2012.
6 Isaac Newton (1642–1727) in *Oxford Dictionary of Quotations*.
7 Richard Dawkins, *The God Delusion*, Black Swan, 2007.

8   Bertrand Russell and Peter Atkins, quoted by Alister McGrath in Chris Jervis et al., *Philosophy, Science and the God Debate* (DVD), 2011.

9   Francis Crick, *The Astonishing Hypothesis: The Scientific Search for the Soul*, Simon & Schuster, 1995.

10 Stephen Hawking and Leonard Mlodinow, *The Grand Design*, Bantam, 2010.

11 *Dara O'Briain Meets Stephen Hawking*, BBC1, June 2015.

12 John C. Lennox, *God and Stephen Hawking*, Lion Books, 2011.

13 Richard Dawkins, *A Devil's Chaplain*, W&N, 2003.

14 Alister McGrath in *Philosophy, Science and the God Debate*.

WEEK 2

Opening quotes:
    Kahlil Gibran, source uncertain.
    Alan Bennett, *Beyond the Fringe*, 1961.

1   Psalm 23:4, *Good News Bible*, The Bible Societies, 1976.

2   Francis Spufford, *Unapologetic: Why, Despite Everything, Christianity Can Still Make Surprising Emotional Sense*, Faber & Faber, 2012.

3   Jane Hawking, *Travelling to Infinity: My Life with Stephen*, Alma Books, 2007.

4   Richard Dawkins, untitled lecture, Edinburgh Science Festival, 1992.

5   Richard Dawkins, *The Selfish Gene*, Oxford University Press, 1976.

6   Søren Kierkegaard, paraphrased by Alister McGrath in *Philosophy, Science and the God Debate*.

7   Keith Ward in Chris Jervis et al., *Philosophy, Science and the God Debate* (DVD), 2011.

8   Alister McGrath in Chris Jervis et al., *Philosophy, Science and the God Debate*.

9   Francis Collins, *The Language of God: A Scientist Presents Evidence for Belief*, Pocket Books, 2007.

10 'List of Christian Thinkers in Science', *Wikipedia*, updated September 2015.

11 Stephen Hawking, *My Brief History*, Bantam Press, 2013.

12 Paul Tillich, *Systematic Theology Vol. 2*, University of Chicago Press, 1957.

13 Sheldon Vanauken, *A Severe Mercy*, quoted in *The Language of God*.

WEEK 3

Opening quotes:

M Scott Peck, *Further Along the Road Less Travelled*, Simon and Schuster, 1993.

Francis Collins interview in *The Sunday Times*, 11 June 2006.

1 Chris Woodhead, quoted by Sian Griffith, 'Ever the Fighter ...', *The Sunday Times*, 28 June 2015.

2 Michael Wenham, *My Donkey Body*, Monarch, 2008.

3 Jane Hawking, *Travelling to Infinity: My Life with Stephen*, Alma Books, 2007.

4 *Ibid*.

5 *Ibid*.

6 John 14:20 and 15:12–16

7 Matthew 10:39.

8 Jane Hawking, *Travelling to Infinity*.

9 M. Scott Peck, *The Road Less Travelled*, Rider, 1978.

10 Francis Collins, *The Language of God*, Pocket Books, 2007.

11 J. R. Lucas, *Wilberforce and Huxley: A Legendary Encounter*, 1979 http://users.ox.ac.uk/~jrlucas/legend.html.

12 Alister McGrath in Chris Jervis et al., *Philosophy, Science and the God Debate* (DVD), 2011.

13 Stephen Hawking, *A Brief History of Time*, Bantam, 1988.

14 Stephen Hawking and Leonard Mlodinow, *The Grand Design*, Bantam, 2010.

15 John C. Lennox, *God and Stephen Hawking*, Lion, 2011.

16 Stephen Hawking, *My Brief History*, Bantam, 2013.

WEEK 4

Opening quotes:

Henry Ford, quoted in *Magazine of Business*, 1927.

Dietrich Bonhoeffer, *Letters and Papers from Prison*, SCM, 1953.

1 Office of National Statistics, figures for 2011 and 2012.

2 Frances Spufford, *Unapologetic*, Faber and Faber, 2012.

3 Barack Obama interviewed by Cathleen Falsani, 'Barack Obama and the God Factor' https://sojo.net/articles/barrack-obama-and-god-factor-interview, 2004.

4   Terry Pratchett, *Carpe Jugulum,* Corgi, 1998.
5   Jane Hawking, *Travelling to Infinity: My Life with Stephen*, Alma Books, 2007.
6   *Ibid*.
7   *Ibid*.
8   Richard Rohr, *Falling Upward,* SPCK, 2012.
9   Luke 18:9–14.
10   Matthew 23.
11   John 8:1–11.
12   Matthew 7:1–5, 12.
13   Stephen Hawking, *A Brief History of Time,* Bantam, 1988.
14   Michel Quoist, *Prayers of Life,* Gill & Son, 1963.
15   Richard of Chichester, from *The Oxford Book of Prayer*, ed: George Appleton, OUP, 1985.
16   Stephen Hawking, *A Brief History of Time*.
17   Michael Wenham, *Diary of a Dancing Donkey*, http://mydonkeybody.blogspot.co.uk.

WEEK 5

Opening quotes:
    Mother Teresa, source unknown.
    'Opinionated Vicar', david.keen.blogspot.co.uk.
1   *Dara O'Briain Meets Stephen Hawking,* BBC1, June 2015 (answer partially recycled from a previous interview).
2   C. S. Lewis, *The Four Loves*, Geoffrey Bles, 1960.
3   Jane Hawking, *Travelling to Infinity: My Life with Stephen*, Alma Books, 2007.
4   Michael Wenham, *My Donkey Body*, Monarch, 2008.
5   Luke 10:27.
6   Stephen and Jane separated in 1990 after 25 years of marriage. They divorced in 1995 and the same year he married Elaine Mason. Two years later Jane and Jonathan were married. There were some accusations in following years that Stephen was physically abused by Elaine, but Stephen refused to bring a complaint and these were never substantiated. They divorced quietly in 2006 and he now lives alone with nursing staff to care for him.
7   Michael Wenham, *My Donkey Body*.
8   Quoted in Tim Adams, 'Jane Hawking: Brief History of a First Wife, *Observer*, April 2004.
9   Colossians 2:2–3 in *The Message* translation.

10 Matthew Henry, quoted by Philip Yancey in *What's so Amazing about Grace?*, Zondervan, 1997.

11 Yancey, *What's so Amazing about Grace?*

12 Stephen Hawking, *A Brief History of Time*, Bantam, 1988.

13 Fred Crix, *Letters from Grandad* (unpublished manuscript), 1998.

14 Steve Chalke, *The Lost Message of Jesus,* Zondervan, 2004.

15 2 Corinthians 12:9.

CONCLUSION

1 Joseph Komonchak et al. (eds), *The New Dictionary of Theology,* Gill & McMillan, 1990.

2 John 3:8.

3 Carl Sagan, Introduction to original edition of Stephen Hawking, *A Brief History of Time*, Bantam, 1988.

BIBLE READINGS

Opening quotes:
    Galileo Galilei, in Stillman Drake, *Discoveries and Opinions of Galileo,* Doubleday, 1957.
    Anonymous Preface to all Gideon New Testaments.

1 1 Timothy 3:16, New International Version.

2 It is true that in 2010 Dr Craig Venter and his team produced the first synthetic cells, capable of multiplying and therefore described as a 'life form'. It was not, however, creating matter out of nothing.

3 Attributed to a number of sources: Sioux legend, Donald Coggan, Gary Zukav etc.

4 New International Version.

5 Anonymous, 'The Loom of Time'.

6 The word 'scientist' was coined by William Whewell in 1833 at the annual meeting of the British Association for the Advancement of Science. Before then they were called 'natural philosophers'.

LEADER'S NOTES

1 Jane Hawking, *Travelling to Infinity: My Life with Stephen*, Alma Books, 2007.

2 *Ibid.*

3 Stephen Hawking, *A Brief History of Time*, Bantam, 1988.

RECOMMENDED RESOURCES

BOOKS

Edgar Andrews, *Who Made God? Searching for a Theory of Everything*, EP Books, 2009.

Francis Collins, *The Language of God: A Scientist Presents Evidence for Belief*, Pocket Books, 2007.

John C. Lennox, *God and Stephen Hawking: Whose Design is It Anyway?*, Lion Books, 2011.

Alister McGrath, *Surprised by Meaning: Science, Faith and How We Make Sense of Things*, WJK Books, 2011.

Russell Stannard, *Science and Belief: The Big Issues*, Lion Books, 2012.

DVD

Chris Jervis, John Lennox, Alister McGrath and Keith Ward, *Philosophy, Science and the God Debate*, Christian Television Association, 2011, http://cta.uk.com/shop?cid=21&pid=195
Eight 20-minute programmes discussing issues of science and faith. Could make an excellent group follow-on resource.